PURE
PLAIN
FLOUR

THE GREAT NEW ZEALAND Baking book

The Great New Zealand Baking Book

CREATED BY Murray Thom & Tim Harper

PHOTOGRAPHY Lottie Hedley **HEAD BAKER** Michelle Pattison **COVER ART** Dick Frizzell

thom & PQ Blackwell

CONTENTS

'Boil whole oranges for two hours...'

And right there, with those first six words, I was stumped. Do you peel the oranges or leave the skin on? It didn't say. *Surely* boiling a peeled orange for two hours wouldn't work, so I elected to put them in whole – just like it said to do, having read the recipe again.

I had got to this stage of my life having never baked a single thing, so it was high time to give something a go and I settled on Shaun Clouston's Orange Cake because it had just five ingredients. I went to the supermarket and bought them in the order they appeared on the recipe:

2 oranges

6 eggs

225 g sugar

225 g ground almonds

1 tsp baking powder

I was about to bake my very first cake.

It probably took me about an hour to get the mix ready; by the time I had 'lightly whisked the eggs and sugar together' and mixed in my puréed oranges (definitely the right decision not to peel them) and having pre-heated the oven to 150°C it was time to pop it in.

What now?

I then pulled up a chair and sat right in front of the oven door in order to watch it cook through the window – I am not kidding, I didn't move for the entire forty minutes.

The result? An absolute triumph!

The Great New Zealand Baking Book handpicks a few favourite recipes made famous from *The Great New Zealand Cookbook* (like the orange cake) and adds over one hundred brand new recipes – the result is an original and inspiring collection of recipes from New Zealand's finest bakers.

I want to give a standing ovation to our sixty fabulous contributors, who have all come on board with such enthusiasm and generosity. A huge thanks to you all for sharing your amazing recipes and stories with us so that we can follow your lead and turn out our own versions of your delicious creations. You guys are the best, and for my part, I am ready for you to guide me through my next baking adventure.

Here's to flour power!

Enjoy,

Murray Thom

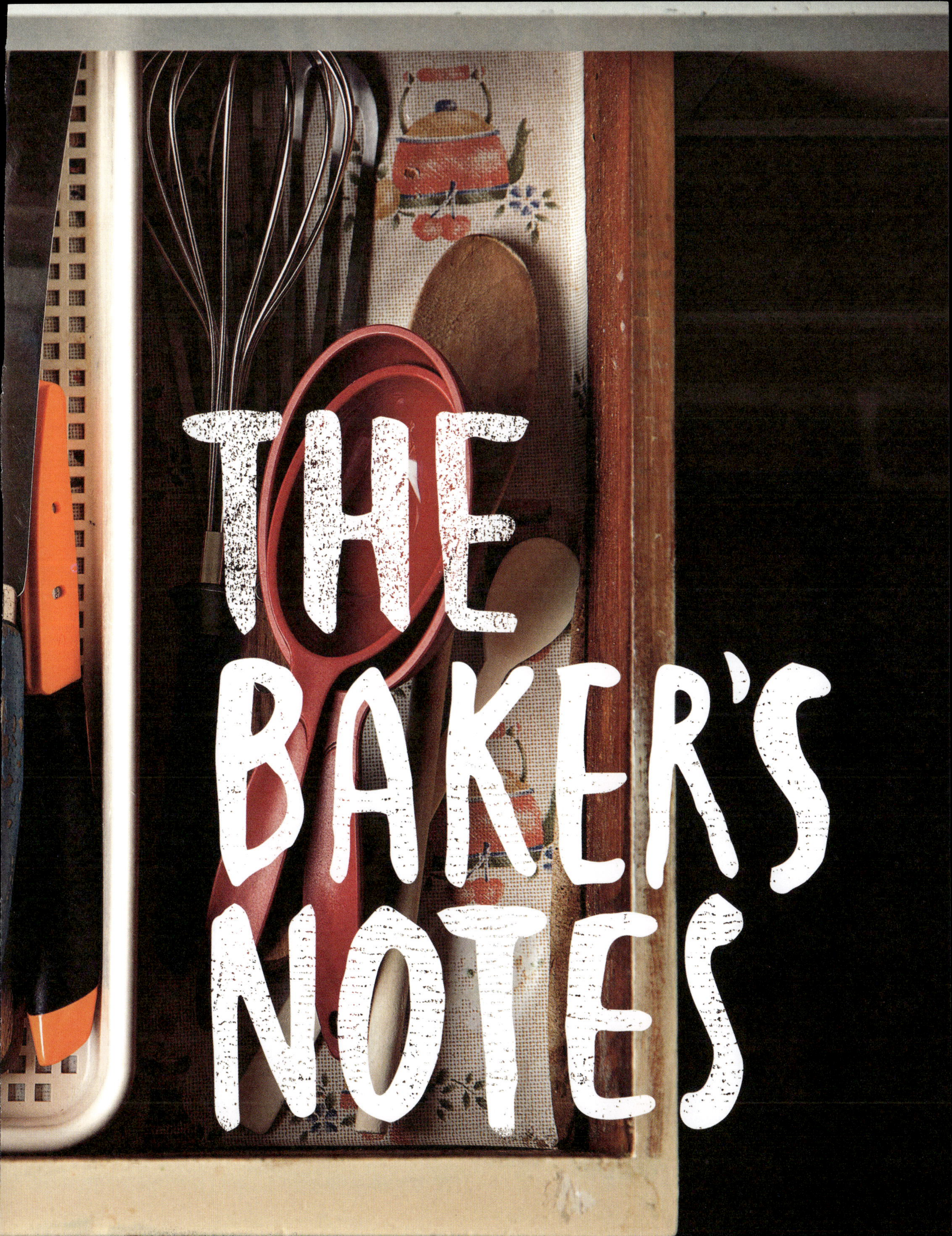

THE BAKER'S NOTES

BEFORE YOU BAKE

I was lucky enough to be brought up in a 'foodie' family. My earliest memories were in the kitchen with either my mother or gran. Qualifying as a chef dotted all my i's and crossed all my t's. All the things I had previously been taught were now explained technically and suddenly everything made sense. Baking is about science and ratios. It relies on exact measurements, ingredients and using the appropriate, clean tools to get perfect results. The principles of baking were passed down to me and I love nothing more than teaching these secrets to others – here's what I've learnt on my journey...

THE PRINCIPLES OF BAKING

There are some fundamental secrets in baking, and once you understand these you'll have more freedom to make and adapt recipes with success. Every ingredient in your baking has at least one function, and these functions need to be in balance with one another.

- **Stabilisers** – stabilising ingredients contain a protein that gives your baking 'structure'. Gluten is the protein in flour, which is important in making bread. This is why it can be challenging to create gluten-free recipes – you need to replace the gluten with something that will give the baking that structure. Often, buckwheat and tapioca are used as gluten-free alternatives.
- **Tenderisers** – these are baking 'fats', which can include butter, oil and lard, as well as other ingredients like cream, milk, buttercream, peanut butter and egg yolk.
- **Sweeteners** – sugar is often used to add a sweet flavour, but sweeteners can also improve structure and stability (the sugar in a meringue does this). Sweeteners also attract moisture to your baking. In this day and age we are using a greater variety of sweeteners, including maple syrup, honey and fruit juices.
- **Leaveners** – these introduce carbon dioxide into your baking, giving you great texture (often light, risen and soft). There are three types of leaveners used in baking: chemical (baking soda, baking powder, etc.); organic (yeast-based, often used for bread); and physical – steam (creating air pockets which cause the layers in steamed buns, steamed puddings, Danishes and puff pastry to separate and rise), and air (incorporated into batters physically through whipping and creaming).
- **Flavourings** – flavours shouldn't change the characteristics of your baking. They can include chocolate, nuts, citrus zests, fruits and essences.
- **Thickeners** – ingredients used to thicken your baking include cornflour, eggs, gelatine, tapioca and arrowroot.

READ YOUR RECIPE

There's nothing that prepares you more than reading your recipe through at least once before you cook. It eliminates surprises like discovering in the middle of baking that you haven't got all the ingredients, the right equipment or enough time. I also like to make notes in my recipes as I go, checking off each ingredient and process. I mark any changes that I make to the recipe to help me remember the next time I cook it.

MISE EN PLACE

One of the first things we were taught at chef school was 'mise en place'. This is a culinary term that simply means 'putting in place' – preparing everything before you start so that you're organised. In a commercial or professional situation this is essential. When you're cooking at home, mise en place will help you feel organised and increase the likelihood of your success – who doesn't want that?

EQUIPMENT

The huge range of kitchen gadgets out there today is all very tempting, but I would recommend getting a few good-quality basics rather than having a kitchen full of stuff that you might never use. My gran built up her equipment over a lifetime and because it was good-quality it was able to be passed on. One of my favourite things from my gran is her rolling pin. It's done a lot of work and is still going strong (you can see it pictured in the leek and cheese tart recipe on page 296). Equipment should, as far as possible, be scrupulously clean, particularly when baking things like meringues or sponges.

Here are the things I'd consider good-quality basics:

- **Electronic scales** – I can't recommend strongly enough the investment in an electronic set of scales. Their price has come down and you can even find them in some supermarkets. Because baking is a science, a difference of even 5 grams of an ingredient can mean the making or breaking of your recipe. If you use cup measurements it's important they're accurate –a lot of measuring cups aren't.
- **Food processor** – a good food processor makes all the difference in your recipes with its slicing and dicing. It also makes light work of mixing doughs. When buying, check the power of the motor and get a good brand – ask your friends how good they find their food processors.
- **Electric mixer** – an electric stand mixer is my personal favourite in the kitchen. I make a huge amount of doughs, creamed sugar and butter, and meringues, and have attachments (like a juicer) that extend the mixer's usefulness. Once again, check the power of the motor. Because I am a chef and do a lot of baking, I went for a top-of-the-line machine, but I had to wait many years for it as it was very expensive. A good food processor will do most things, and is a good start while you save up. I would also recommend getting a mixer that can be serviced. My mixer became a bit squeaky at one point but was like new after servicing.
- **Basic tools** – to me the basic equipment in your kitchen would include measuring cups and spoons, a sieve, a whisk, a spatula, a wooden spoon, a pastry brush, a zester, a good-quality chef's knife and lots of little sharp knives, mixing bowls, saucepans (with good bases), and baking tins and trays.
- **Other electric gadgets** – lastly, I would recommend having an electric hand-mixer and an electric blender (good for blending soups and sauces).

PREPARE YOUR TINS

'Prepare your tin' is a term frequently used by chefs. It simply means 'grease your tin and line it with baking paper' or 'grease and flour your tin'. This preparation minimises the chances of your baking sticking as you turn it out onto a cooling rack.

Here are some tips on choosing and preparing tins:

- **Tin type** – I prefer tins to ceramic dishes, particularly when baking cakes and pastries. Your baking batters will tend to cook better because tin allows the heat through better. This means you are more likely to get a golden base on your baking rather than a soggy bottom.
- **Tin sizes** – it's important to use the correct tin size when you're baking, as using the wrong sized tin can alter the final result.
- **Brioche tins** – these are sold individually and can be found in specialty cooking stores. They give a very pretty fluted look to your baking. A muffin tin can be used as an alternative.
- **Oil spray** – I like to use an oil spray for greasing my tins and I'm pretty generous when I spray: it's so disheartening if a piece of cake separates itself when being turned out.
- **Tinfoil** – I sometimes line my tart tins or springform cake tins with tinfoil rather than baking paper. Tinfoil is a lot less bulky than paper and easier to work with when preparing your tins.
- **DIY muffin cup cases** – I like to make my own muffin cup cases out of baking paper. It's easy to do, and looks just like the muffin cases in cafés. Simply cut out baking paper squares to 12 cm x 12 cm (standard muffin tins) or 14 cm x 14 cm (large muffin tins). Press the centre of each square down into the centre of the muffin hole (it will naturally crease around the edges). Press the creases firmly and the paper case will hold its shape. Easy!
- **Baking trays** – when using baking trays I make sure they are greased, lined and cool. If you put biscuit batter on a hot tray it can melt the batter and the biscuits' shape is lost as a result – I find this particularly true with Anzac biscuits.

PRE-HEAT YOUR OVEN

Believe it or not, a pre-heated oven can make all the difference with baking. If you've gone to the trouble of whipping things up so that they are light and fluffy and then you have to sit them on the bench for 15 minutes until the oven reaches temperature, your baking could flatten.

Note that a lot of ovens these days have a 'fan-bake' setting. It's often best not to use this with general baking because it can cook unevenly. If you do use fan-bake, you'll need to reduce the temperature given in the recipe by 20°C.

BASIC INGREDIENTS FOR BAKING

There are a number of key ingredients that you'll see over and over again in baking recipes.

FLOURS

- **High-grade** – a strong white flour with a high gluten content. Its main use is for making bread and puff pastry.
- **Plain (standard) flour** – a soft white flour with a lower gluten content than high-grade. Its main use is for cakes, biscuits, slices, etc. A raising agent (leavener) may need to be added.
- **Self-raising flour** – a soft white flour with a raising agent (leavener) incorporated into it. It's mainly used for cakes. If you run out of self-raising flour, you can mix up your own: in general, use 1 teaspoon of baking powder to 1 cup of plain flour and sift them together before using.
- **Buckwheat flour** – not a wheat-based flour, this is often used as a gluten-free flour substitute.
- **Other flours** – a lot of non-wheat products are described as flours or meals, e.g. almond flour/almond meal. The word 'flour' can refer to the texture. If a recipe calls for (for example) cashew flour, you can simply put cashew nuts in your food processor and grind them until they have a flour-like consistency. Be careful not to process beyond this point because it could turn into a paste or butter.

FATS

- **Butter** – this is used at room temperature unless you're making pastry (in which case you chill it). Our New Zealand butter is quite yellow, and can have disappointing results when making coloured icings. Compared with other fats, butter can be less stable at room temperature because it might melt or not hold its shape as well.
- **Oils** – oils have different flavours. For baking, you generally use an oil with no distinguishable flavour, e.g. grapeseed oil.

Every oil has a different burning point, which should be higher than the temperature you will cook it at. Grapeseed and canola oil have high burning points. Extra virgin olive oil has a very low burning point, so is generally only used when cooking isn't required.

If you're unsure which oil to use for a recipe, take a minute to read the labels on the bottles when you visit the store – they often recommend the appropriate cooking method. If you're still unsure, ask someone in the store for advice.

EGGS

- As a rule, fresh eggs will last for two weeks at room temperature and two months refrigerated (or as the label on the eggs suggests). Be careful, as this can vary greatly depending on the environment the egg has been in. Try to store your room-temperature eggs in a cool, dark place. To test whether your eggs are OK, put them in a bowl of cold water – each egg should sink to the bottom. If they float to the top they have gone bad; gas has got into the egg and spoilt it.
- Use fresh eggs in baking – unless you're making meringues, where it's preferable to have eggs 7–10 days old. A pinch of salt can strengthen egg whites, which can also be helpful when making meringues.
- Use eggs at room temperature unless making pastry (then use them chilled). I generally store my eggs in the refrigerator, taking them out an hour or so before I bake to let them come to room temperature.
- A size 6 (standard) egg weighs about 50 grams (20 grams yolk and 30 grams white), and is good for most recipes. If a recipe asks for ½ egg or gives a gram weight, simply break the egg into a small bowl, lightly whisk the yolk and white together and weigh to get the amount you need.
- When you have large quantities of eggs that need to be separated (i.e. separate the yolks from the whites), it's a good idea to use several bowls. Break each egg over a small bowl and collect the white, then transfer the white to a larger bowl and the yolk to a third bowl. If you accidentally break some yolk into the white when separating, the white needs to be discarded. It would be devastating if you did this after separating 10 eggs between just two bowls!
- Egg-wash means brushing your baking with an egg that's been whisked up, to give your baking a protective seal and a nice golden colour. A splash of water whisked

in with the egg prevents it becoming too thick and coagulating (becoming solid and cooked) – you want egg-wash to set nicely in more of a liquid state.

SUGARS

- Sugar is generally used as a flavour and shouldn't affect the behaviour of the batter. Most cakes require standard sugar, but there are a lot of alternatives used these days (e.g. maple syrup or honey).
- Caster sugar is often used when the sugar needs to dissolve quickly, i.e. when creaming or making meringues.
- Icing sugar is usually used for icing.
- Brown, raw or coconut sugar is used when you are wanting a deeper or a more natural flavour.
- Cooking sugar can create amazing effects. It's important to work quickly, have all your equipment ready and use a candy thermometer because there's a big difference even in 1°C at high heats.

SALT

Use table salt unless stated otherwise. Maldon sea salt is sometimes called for. This is a natural, flaky salt from the sea and isn't as concentrated in flavour as table salt.

BAKING METHODS

MEASUREMENT AND PREPARATION

When you follow the recipe instructions/methods, remember to think about:

- **Weighing/measuring** – carefully weigh each ingredient in order. Measuring cups are often marked in increments of 50 grams (g) or millilitres (ml). If the measurement is in between the 50 marks, use measuring spoons to add up to the amount you are after. Note that brown sugar is often called for as 'packed', which means you press the sugar down in the measuring cup to get the right amount. If using measuring spoons, always level dry ingredients off with a knife.

  As a rough guide:

  250 g/ml = 1 cup

  125 g/ml = ½ cup

  65 g/ml = ¼ cup

  15 g/ml = 1 tablespoon

  5 g/ml = 1 teaspoon
- **Chopping** – cutting food into pieces, usually done with a large, sharp chef's knife. When doing the chopping action I hold the tip of the knife down on the board with my left hand and hold the handle of the knife in my right hand. Finely chopped food is in very small pieces – almost grain size; roughly chopped is more like bite-sized pieces.
- **Straining/sifting** – using a sieve to prevent any lumps or sediment from being added to your batter. Sifting also helps to get air into the mixture.
- **Folding** – mixing ingredients carefully with a spoon or hands without losing air.
- **Creaming** – working butter and sugar together (usually with an electric mixer) to create a smooth, light, often fluffy paste.
- **Toasting** – toasting coconut or nuts adds a lovely depth of flavour and colour to baking. It's simple to do: just place the coconut or nuts in a shallow baking tray in an oven pre-heated to 175°C – not fan-bake. Bake for 3–5 minutes, turning or shaking regularly, until lightly golden. Watch closely – check every minute because it can burn quickly. Cool your coconut or nuts before adding to your baking.

OVEN TIPS

KEY POINTS TO REMEMBER

- Individual ovens all vary in the way they heat. Be mindful of this – you don't know what type of oven the recipe writer has used. It might be a commercial oven, which is a lot more powerful than your domestic oven. It might be gas, where you have electric. Use the baking times and temperatures as a guide and get to know how your oven works.
- As a rule, pour your mixture into the tin until it's two-thirds full. This allows for the rising of your baking. I often use a scraper to carefully smooth the top of the batter evenly as well.

- You can bake with multiple trays in the oven, but make sure it's the same recipe – don't mix different baked goods in one oven. If you have two baking trays in the one oven, it's often a good idea to swap their positions in the oven about three-quarters of the way through cooking so that they come out cooked about the same.
- Baking is best put in the middle of the oven, which gives an even distribution of heat. If you know you want more heat on the bottom of your baking, put it on a lower shelf; if you want it more golden on top, raise it to a higher shelf.
- Don't be tempted to open the oven door until it's about three-quarters of the way through the cooking time, to prevent your baking from sinking. Set the timer for less than the recipe says (say 5–10 minutes, depending on the recipe), then keep adjusting the timer to 3– to 5–minute intervals until you are sure it's cooked.
- If you know your baking isn't cooked through but it's looking golden on top already, carefully place a sheet of tinfoil on top. This will stop it getting any darker on top but will allow it to continue cooking until it's fully done.
- One of the easiest ways to test whether your baking is cooked is to press down gently on it with your finger; if it's relatively firm and bounces back, it should be done. You can also insert a metal skewer into the centre – if it comes out clean, it should be ready. Be careful using this second method with delicate items, because it lets precious air escape.

AFTER YOU BAKE

- Be gentle when bringing your baking out of the oven. It can be affected by the change in temperature, being knocked, etc., until it's completely cooled.
- Leave baking in/on the tin for approximately 3 minutes for muffins and biscuits and 10 minutes for a loaf or cake, before turning it out. Turning out simply means turning your baking upside down onto (usually) a cake rack. I also run a knife gently around the inside edge of the tin to loosen any part of the cake that might have stuck. A gentle tap on the top of the tin while turning it out can also help if it's taking a while to release itself. A lined baking tin makes this process a lot simpler (see notes about preparing tins).
- Cool all baking completely before icing/decorating. Just a little warmth remaining in your baking can ruin your icing.
- Most cakes and loaves freeze well. Wrap the completely cooled cake/loaf in tinfoil first (which prevents it from drying out) and then in plastic wrap. Ice it after defrosting. To defrost baking, bring it back to room temperature slowly (still wrapped), either in the refrigerator or on the bench.

Last but not least, while I have made and tested the recipes you find here, don't be afraid to have fun with your baking. The more you bake the better you'll get to know the basic methods and processes, and before you know it you'll find yourself experimenting with flavours and ingredients to create your own personal favourites.

Good luck and happy baking!

Michelle Pattison

THE COOK'S COMPANION

CLOSE-ENOUGH CONVERSIONS

LIQUID/VOLUME

1 TBSP	½ FL OZ	3 TSP	15 ML
2 TBSP	1 FL OZ	6 TSP	30 ML
¼ CUP	2 FL OZ	4 TBSP	65 ML
⅓ CUP	2½ FL OZ	5 TBSP	75 ML
½ CUP	4 FL OZ	8 TBSP	125 ML
⅔ CUP	5 FL OZ	10 TBSP	150 ML
¾ CUP	6 FL OZ	12 TBSP	175 ML
1 CUP	8 FL OZ	16 TBSP	250 ML
1¼ CUPS	10 FL OZ		310 ML
1½ CUPS	12 FL OZ		350 ML
1 PINT (2 CUPS)	16 FL OZ		500 ML
2½ CUPS	20 FL OZ		625 ML
1 QUART	32 FL OZ		1 LITRE
1 GALLON	128 FL OZ		4 LITRES

DRY/WEIGHT

¼ OZ	7 G
½ OZ	15 G
1 OZ	30 G
2 OZ	55 G
3 OZ	85 G
4 OZ	115 G
5 OZ	140 G
6 OZ	170 G
7 OZ	200 G
8 OZ (½ LB)	225 G
9 OZ	255 G
10 OZ	285 G
11 OZ	310 G
12 OZ	340 G
13 OZ	370 G
14 OZ	400 G
15 OZ	425 G
16 OZ (1 LB)	450 G

TEMPERATURE

VERY COOL	275°F	140°C
COOL	300°F	150°C
WARM	325°F	160°C
MEDIUM	350°F	180°C
MEDIUM HOT	400°F	200°C
HOT	425°F	220°C
VERY HOT	450°F	240°C

FRIZZELL/14

DOUGH & PASTRY BASICS

BRIOCHE DOUGH *Recipe by* **LITTLE & FRIDAY**

MAKES: 1 LARGE QUANTITY DOUGH | PREP TIME: 40–50 MINS | SKILL LEVEL: 2 (MODERATE)

INGREDIENTS

550 ml milk
60 g fresh yeast (crumbled) or 3 tsp dry yeast
½ cup sugar
6½ cups plain flour
3 tsp salt
3 eggs
140 g unsalted butter

METHOD

Heat milk over a medium heat until lukewarm. Remove from heat and pour over yeast, stirring until yeast has dissolved.

Place dry ingredients in a mixing bowl. Using an electric mixer with a dough hook, mix at low speed (or mix by hand) to combine fully. Add milk/yeast mixture and eggs to the bowl, continuing to mix at low speed until a sticky dough forms. Stop the mixer. Scrape down the dough and then turn the mixer speed on to medium for 10 minutes until an elastic, shiny dough forms and pulls away from the bowl. If doing this by hand, knead the dough on a lightly floured surface.

Cut butter into small pieces and gradually knead into the mixture until well combined. Cover the bowl with a tea towel and allow dough to rise until almost doubled in size. Tip dough onto a floured surface. It is now ready to use.

TIPS

Traditional brioche recipes require the dough to be chilled prior to it being used – overnight or for at least 2 hours. I tend to avoid this as the dough comes out slightly firmer and less fluffy. My method means you have to work faster once the dough is ready, to stop it from over-rising, especially during summer. If it rises too quickly, place it in the refrigerator for short periods to slow down the process.

DANISH PASTRY DOUGH *Recipe by* **THE CLAREVILLE BAKERY**

MAKES: 1 LARGE QUANTITY DOUGH | PREP TIME: 45 MINS, PLUS FERMENTING & CHILLING | SKILL LEVEL: 3 (CHALLENGING)

INGREDIENTS

500 g '00' or bakers flour
50 g caster sugar
2 tsp salt
20 g butter
1 tsp (6 g) yeast
250 ml cold milk
1 egg
250 g butter for rolling

METHOD

Prepare dough the day before using. Place all dough ingredients (except butter for rolling) in a mixing bowl and use your hands to combine them all together into a rough mass. Tip mass onto a clean work surface and knead for 12–15 minutes. The dough should be developed and kneaded till it is smooth and elastic. Every couple of minutes, take 30 seconds rest – the dough will be quite firm, but don't be tempted to add more liquid to it as then it will be too soft later on. Once dough is fully kneaded, place in a lightly oiled container and allow to ferment at room temperature for 1 hour. Cover and chill in the refrigerator overnight.

Place extra butter between two sheets of plastic wrap and use a rolling pin to knock the butter into a square 1 cm thick (approximately 15 cm x 15 cm). Chill (it needs to be firm but malleable).

The next day, tip dough onto a lightly floured work surface and roll into a square 1 cm thick (approximately 25 cm x 25 cm). Place butter onto dough with the corners of the butter just inside the straight sides of the dough. Fold the corners of the dough into the centre of the butter, encasing the butter fully. You should now have two layers of dough and one layer of butter inside the dough layers. Roll pastry into a rectangle, to approximately 1–1.5 cm thick. The length should be approximately three times the width. Now imagine the pastry divided into three parts. Fold one end of the pastry two-thirds of the way towards the other end, then fold the other end over the first fold to give three even layers. This is called a 'single turn'.

Cover dough with plastic wrap and chill for 30 minutes. Repeat the rolling and folding and chill for another 30 minutes. Repeat one more time; you should now have given the pastry three single turns. Chill pastry for a further 30 minutes before preparing and assembling for cooking.

ROUGH PUFF PASTRY *Recipe by* **CANTERBURY CHEESEMONGERS**

MAKES: 1,200 G | PREP TIME: 2 HOURS | SKILL LEVEL: 2–3 (MORE CHALLENGING BUT EASIER WITH PRACTICE)

INGREDIENTS

240 g plain flour
240 g high-grade flour
½ tsp salt
480 g butter (cold but not straight from the fridge)
240 g cold water

METHOD

Sift flours and salt together into a mixing bowl and rub in 140 grams of butter until the mixture resembles fine breadcrumbs. Add cold water and stir to form a shaggy dough. Use your hands to push the dough into a ball, then squash this onto a lightly floured work surface and roll into a rectangle approximately 20 cm x 30 cm.

Divide the rest of the butter into eight cubes and flatten each piece between your palms. Place four pieces to cover the middle third of the dough and fold one of the ends over to seal. Cover this with the remaining butter and stretch the last third of dough over to seal.

Rotate pastry so that the short sides are at the top and bottom and roll this out into a rectangle approximately 28 cm x 44 cm. Use a dough scraper or palette knife to help push the pastry into shape. Fold the short ends over to meet in the middle, then fold again as if closing a book. Rotate clockwise so that short ends are at top and bottom. This is your first turn.

Repeat this rolling and folding two more times; you may need to chill the dough in the fridge for 30 minutes after each turn, to keep it cool and not sticky. Be gentle with your rolling out and remember to sprinkle a little flour on your work surface and rolling pin each time.

Do one final turn, but instead of folding your dough into a book shape, mentally divide it into three, folding the top down to cover the middle third and the bottom up to cover that. Your finished flaky pastry should measure approximately 15 cm x 30 cm and will have had four turns.

One recipe of pastry will be enough for eight Eccles cakes plus four mince and cheese pies.

TIPS

This rough puff pastry is one of those things where the more you do, the easier it gets. If you have a spare Sunday afternoon, make a whole heap and freeze it.

VERY SHORT SHORTCRUST PASTRY

Recipe by **CANTERBURY CHEESEMONGERS**

MAKES: 600 G OR 12 TART BASES | PREP TIME: 15 MINS | SKILL LEVEL: 1 (EASY)

INGREDIENTS

250 g plain flour
70 g cornflour
50 g caster sugar
pinch of salt
220 g butter, at room temperature
1 large egg yolk (reserve white to glaze pastry cases; see (p.208)

METHOD

Sift dry ingredients into a mixing bowl and rub butter in with your fingertips, or use a food processor to combine. The mixture will be a little sticky. Add egg yolk and combine this evenly with a spoon. Push and squeeze the mixture until it just forms a soft dough. Place on a lightly floured work surface and gently flatten into a disc – do not overwork the dough. At this point you can use the pastry immediately, or wrap and chill (or freeze) it to use at a later time.

JIM BYARS

BAKED DESSERTS

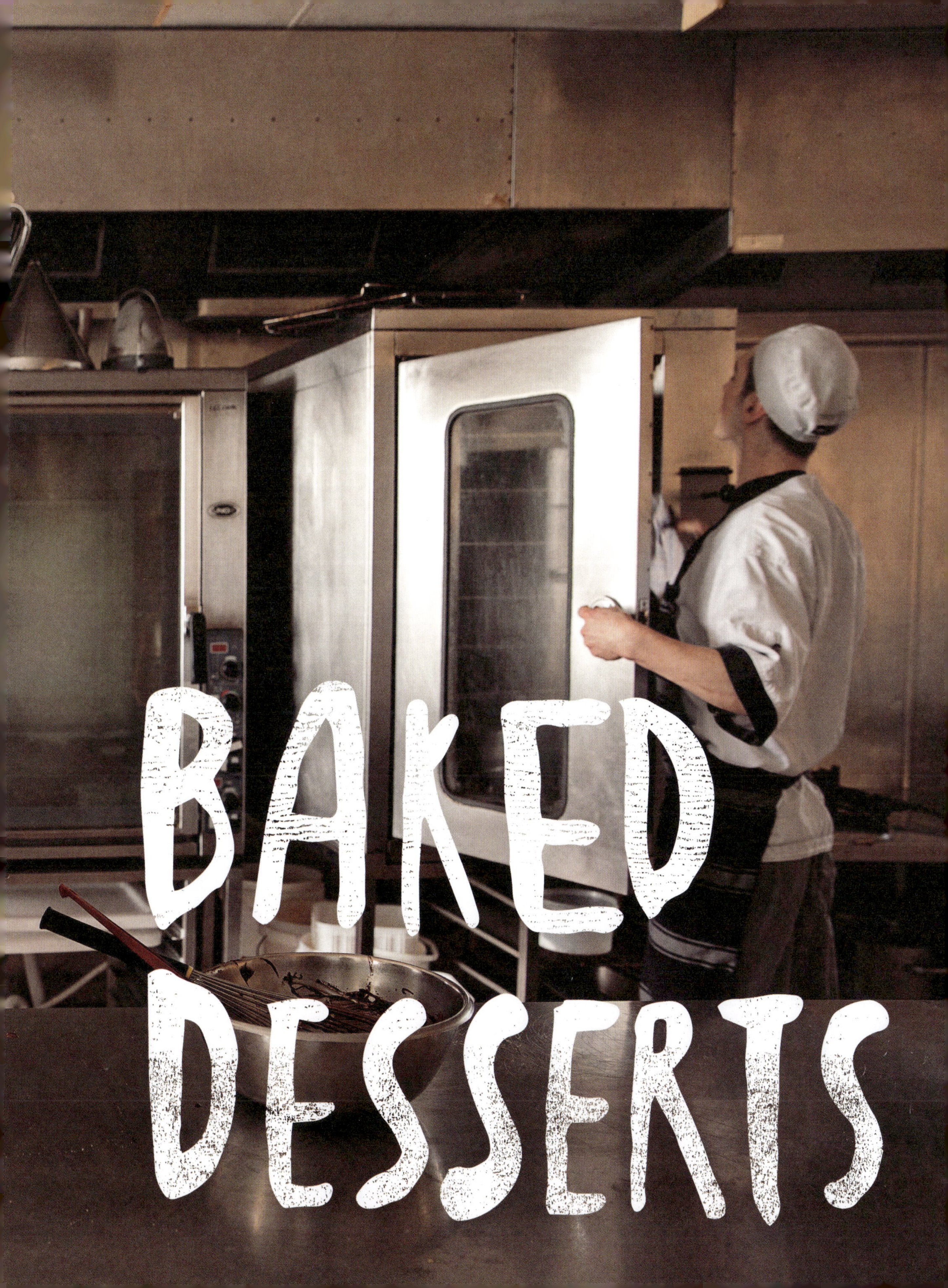

CHOCOLATE TART

Recipe by **JIM BYARS** *from The Friday Shop*

MAKES: 1 LARGE TART | PREP TIME: 15 MINS, PLUS CHILLING COOK TIME: 25–35 MINS | SKILL LEVEL: 2 (MODERATE)

INGREDIENTS

400 g sweet pastry

Filling

200 g dark chocolate
100 g butter
2 egg yolks
1 whole egg
25 g caster sugar

Ganache

200 g dark chocolate, chopped
100 ml cream

METHOD

Pre-heat oven to 200°C (or 165–180°C fan-bake).

Roll pastry out on a floured work surface and use to line a 25 cm flan ring tin, leaving a good overlapping edge. Rest in the fridge for 15 minutes.

Line pastry with greaseproof paper and weigh it down with baking beans. Bake for 20 minutes, then take out of the oven and turn oven down to 170°C (145–150°C fan-bake). Remove paper and beans, and cut off overlapping edge of pastry.

While pastry is baking, melt chocolate and butter in a bowl over a pan of simmering water, whisking until smooth. Cool slightly. Beat egg yolks, whole egg and sugar in a mixer until thick, then mix in chocolate and butter mixture. Put in the pastry shell and bake until set, approximately 10–20 minutes. The filling will feel firm to the touch, with a light crust. Remove from oven.

In the meantime, heat cream in a pan to just under simmering and add chocolate. Whisk until smooth. Pour ganache over the chocolate tart and leave it to set at room temperature.

PAVLOVA

Recipe by **DAME ALISON HOLST**

SERVINGS: 12 | PREP TIME: 20 MINS | COOK TIME: 1 ¾ HOURS | SKILL LEVEL: 1 (EASY)

INGREDIENTS

2 cups (460 g) caster sugar
4 tsp cornflour
½ tsp salt
2 tsp wine vinegar
1 tsp vanilla essence
1 cup (6–8) egg whites

GF

METHOD

Pre-heat the oven to 100°C. Carefully measure sugar, cornflour and salt into a clean, dry bowl with no traces of fat. Stir together.

Add vinegar and vanilla, then measure and add egg whites, taking care to get absolutely no yolk in the mixture. Beat with an electric mixer at high speed for about 20 minutes, until a thick, non-gritty meringue forms. When you lift out the mixer blades, the peaks should stand up stiffly, or just bend over at their tips.

Cover a baking sheet with baking paper, then pile the mixture onto this into a round shape about 25 cm across. Bake for 1 hour and 45 minutes, then turn oven off and leave for 15 minutes longer. Take out of oven after this time.

Leave unwrapped, in a cool place, for up to two days. To serve, top with whipped cream. Decorate traditionally with strawberries, kiwifruit or passionfruit or use other fruit. Drizzle chocolate topping over strawberries if desired.

TIPS

Because ovens vary, cooking times may need to be changed slightly. Pavlovas with a space below the crust and a compacted middle have been cooked too long. If centres are not completely set, cook a little longer next time. Fan-bake for the first 10 minutes if you have this option. If fan-baking for the whole time, lower the temperature by about 10°C.

"Anyone can make this easy recipe. Everything goes into the bowl and then you whip it all up and pop it into the oven."

LEMON MERINGUE PIE

Recipe by **SIMON WRIGHT** *from The French Café*

SERVES: 4–6 | PREP TIME: 35 MINS, PLUS RESTING | COOK TIME: 32 MINS | SKILL LEVEL: 3 (CHALLENGING)

INGREDIENTS

Pastry

225 g plain flour
pinch of salt
60 g caster sugar
150 g cold butter, cut into small cubes
1 egg yolk
25 ml cold water
4 Digestive biscuits, crushed

Lemon filling

zest of 6 lemons
375 ml lemon juice
150 ml water
60 g cornflour
450 g caster sugar
9 egg yolks
75 g butter

Meringue

200 g sugar
100 ml water
4 egg whites
pinch of cream of tartar
30 ml lemon juice
1 lemon

METHOD

For the pie pastry: place the flour, salt and sugar in a food processor and pulse together to mix. Add the butter and pulse until fully incorporated and the mixture resembles fine breadcrumbs. Add the egg yolk and the water, process until the mixture starts to come together and then tip the dough onto a clean work surface and gently knead together. Flatten it slightly with the palm of your hand, wrap in plastic wrap and refrigerate for 1 hour.

Lightly butter and flour a 23 cm by 4 cm pie dish with a removable base. Remove the pastry from the fridge, unwrap it and allow it to soften at room temperature for 10 minutes. Place half of the crushed digestives on a clean work surface, place the pastry on top of the biscuits and roll the pastry out to about 3 cm thick. Sprinkle with the remaining biscuit crumbs and gently press them into the pastry with your rolling pin.

Line your prepared pie tin with the pastry. Roll your rolling pin across the top of the tin to remove excess pastry, then use your thumb and forefinger to crimp around the top of the pie tin so the pastry comes up above the edge. This will allow for a little shrinkage during cooking. Place the prepared pie tin back in the fridge to rest for 30 minutes.

Pre-heat your oven to 180°C. Line the pie tin with baking paper and baking beans and cook for 20 minutes. Remove the paper and beans and return to the oven for another 12 minutes or until the pastry is golden. Remove from the oven and allow the pastry to cool.

For the lemon filling: place the lemon zest, lemon juice and water in a heavy-based saucepan and whisk in the cornflour until the mixture is smooth. Add the sugar and egg yolks and stir until fully incorporated. Place over a medium heat and stir continuously until the mixture is warm, then add the butter and continue to stir until the mixture starts to boil and has thickened. Remove from the heat, pour the lemon filling into your prepared pie case and allow to cool fully at room temperature.

For the meringue: combine the sugar and water in a small saucepan and bring to the boil, stirring continuously with a wooden spoon until the sugar has dissolved. Reduce the heat slightly and continue to cook the syrup without stirring until it reaches 115°C on a sugar thermometer.

Place the egg whites in the bowl of an electric mixer fitted with a whisk attachment, add the cream of tartar and start whisking the egg whites until they reach soft peaks. Once the sugar syrup reaches 120°C, remove from the heat and slowly pour onto the whisking egg whites. Add the lemon juice and continue to beat on a medium speed until the meringue has cooled and is thick and glossy.

Remove the outside ring from the pie tin and place the pie on a serving dish. Spoon the meringue on top of the lemon filling, shaping it so it looks dramatic with spikes and curls. Finely grate the zest of the lemon over the meringue and carefully brown the meringue using a blowtorch. If you don't have a blowtorch, you can remove the meringue from the pie ring and place it under a hot oven grill to brown – this will take a matter of seconds.

CHOCOLATE ROULADE

Recipe by **RUTH PRETTY** *from Ruth Pretty Catering*

SERVES: 8–10 | PREP TIME: 1 HOUR, PLUS COOLING & CHILLING | COOK TIME: 17 MINS | SKILL LEVEL: 2 (MODERATE)

INGREDIENTS

Cake

135 g dark chocolate, preferably 70% cocoa solids (buttons, or tablet chopped coarsely)

35 ml strong freshly brewed coffee

5 eggs, separated

135 g caster sugar

pinch of salt

Mousse

125 g dark chocolate, preferably 70% cocoa solids (buttons, or tablet chopped coarsely)

60 g full-fat cream cheese, coarsely chopped

70 g caster sugar

1 egg yolk

300 ml cream

Ganache

315 ml cream

315 g dark chocolate, preferably 70% cocoa solids (buttons, or tablet coarsely chopped)

50 g butter

METHOD

Make the cake and mousse one or two days ahead, then make the ganache and assemble on the day you wish to serve.

To make cake: pre-heat oven to 180°C. Line a sponge-roll tin with baking paper and grease the paper with spray oil or melted butter.

Place chocolate and coffee in a double boiler or a heatproof bowl, set over a pot of simmering water, and warm over a medium heat until chocolate begins to melt. Remove from the heat and stir until chocolate is completely liquid.

Place egg yolks in a bowl and whisk briefly, then gradually add sugar, continuing to whisk until the mixture is pale, fluffy and very thick. Add warm chocolate mixture and salt to egg yolk mixture and whisk until cool.

To a clean bowl, add egg whites and whisk until stiff peaks form. Carefully fold half the beaten whites into the chocolate mixture, and when almost combined add the remaining half and fold in. Pour mixture into prepared tin and spread evenly. Bake for 15–17 minutes, or until the cake springs back when gently touched in the centre.

Remove cake from oven and place on a wire rack. Cover with plastic wrap and let cool for 1 hour. Invert the cake, leaving the plastic wrap in place, and carefully peel away the baking paper.

To make mousse: place chocolate in a double boiler or a heatproof bowl, set over a pot of simmering water, and warm over a low heat. Stir chocolate until it is almost melted. Cool.

Whip cream until it forms soft peaks. Set aside.

Place cream cheese, sugar and egg yolk in the bowl of a food processor fitted with a metal blade, and process until mixture is smooth and sugar is dissolved. Pour chocolate through the feed tube of the food processor and process until mixture is just combined. Quickly transfer the chocolate mixture to a large bowl and gently fold in cream. Chill for at least 2 hours, or overnight, before using.

To make ganache: place cream and chocolate in a double boiler set over a low heat or a heatproof bowl set over a pot of simmering water, and let it sit for 1 minute. Stir gently until chocolate is half-melted. Remove from heat and continue to stir until chocolate is melted, fully amalgamated and smooth. You may need to return pot to heat to encourage melting of the chocolate. Add butter and stir until melted and ganache is smooth. Rest at room temperature for 15–20 minutes or until it sets to a soft butter-like consistency.

To assemble: spread cake with chocolate mousse. Carefully roll the cake up from one long side, lifting the plastic wrap to get it started. Place the roll, seam-side down, and chill for at least 1 hour, or overnight, before icing with ganache.

Place roulade on a serving tray and use a palette knife or table knife to spread chocolate ganache onto roulade. Do not apply water or heat to the spreader, as the ganache will become streaky and discoloured.

HUMMINGBIRD BOMBE ALASKA

Recipe by **ANDREW & JULIA CLARKE** *from Victoria Street Bistro*

MAKES: 1 | PREP TIME: 40 MINS | COOK TIME: 25 MINS | SKILL LEVEL: 2 (MODERATE)

INGREDIENTS

Hummingbird cake

- 5 or 6 medium-sized bananas (2 cups when crushed)
- 3 cups gluten-free flour
- 1 tsp salt
- 1 tsp baking soda
- 2 tsp ground cinnamon
- 1 cup white sugar
- 1 cup brown sugar
- 1 tbsp vanilla extract
- 3 eggs
- ½ cup canola oil
- ½ cup olive oil
- 1 cup (100 g) chopped pecan nuts
- 1 cup crushed pineapple (drained well)

Raw-sugar meringue

- 1 cup (about 7) egg whites
- 2 cups raw sugar
- 1 tbsp vanilla extract

To assemble

- ¼ cup (50 g) roughly chopped pecan nuts
- ¼ cup (35 g) pumpkin seeds
- ¼ cup (35 g) poppy seeds
- ¼ cup (35 g) sunflower seeds
- 1 litre good-quality vanilla bean or mascarpone ice cream

GF

METHOD

For the cake: pre-heat oven to 180°C. Place whole bananas on a baking tray and roast for 10 minutes, then cool. When cool enough to handle, peel and crush using the back of a fork.

Turn oven down to 170°C. Line a baking tray with baking paper.

Sift together flour, salt, baking soda and cinnamon. In a separate bowl, beat together sugars, vanilla and eggs until thick and creamy. Whisk oils into egg mixture. Add dry ingredients all at once and stir to incorporate, then add pecans, pineapple and banana and stir until combined.

Spread mixture onto lined baking tray about 3 cm thick, and bake for around 20 minutes until done. Cool on the tray for 15 minutes, then transfer to a wire rack and place in the fridge to chill.

For the meringue: place all ingredients in a large metal bowl, place over a pan of simmering water and whisk continuously until sugar dissolves (around 5 minutes). Transfer to a cake mixer with whisk attachment and whisk on high for around 4 minutes, until meringue is rich and velvety. Place in a piping bag in the freezer until needed.

To assemble: pre-heat oven to 200°C fan-bake (230°C regular bake). Mix nuts and seeds together.

Cut chilled cake in half. Cover one half with a layer of ice cream 3 cm thick and place the other cake half on top. Press down firmly. Cut into 4 cm squares or logs (or whatever shape you like), and place on a tray lined with baking paper. Pipe meringue neatly all over the cakes, sprinkle with nut/seed mix and fan-bake for about 3 minutes, until meringue is cooked but ice cream is not melted. Serve immediately.

TIPS

The bombes can be flambéed at the table for a dramatic effect. Turn down the lights, gently warm a shot or two of Cointreau, set it alight and pour over the top of the dessert (best to use something with a handle). We serve this dessert with poached stone-fruit, but it is great on its own or with a simple crème anglaise. Feel free to mix up the flavours of the ice cream, meringue, liquer or cake – have fun with it.

CHOCOLATE GOLD RUSH FRYPAN BROWNIE

Recipe by **KATE FAY** *from Cibo*

SERVINGS: 6 | PREP TIME: 30 MINS | COOK TIME: 20–30 MINS | SKILL LEVEL: 2 (MODERATE)

INGREDIENTS

Hokey pokey

5 tbsp caster sugar
2 tbsp golden syrup
1 tsp baking soda

Brownie

55 g plain flour, sifted
½ tsp baking powder
½ tsp sea salt
220 g dark chocolate
75 g unsalted butter
4 eggs
120 g caster sugar
85 g soft brown sugar
1 tsp vanilla paste
85 g dark chocolate chips
85 g milk chocolate chips
70 g hokey pokey pieces (or you can use a cut-up Crunchie bar), plus extra to serve
vanilla ice cream, to serve

METHOD

For the hokey pokey: in a saucepan, bring sugar and golden syrup to the boil, slowly stirring slowly all the time as this mixture tends to burn easily. Once at boiling point, reduce the heat and simmer, without stirring, for approximately 4 minutes. Remove the pan from the heat and add baking soda – stir it in quickly as it causes the mixture to froth up. Pour mixture onto a piece of baking paper and set aside to cool. Break into pieces and store in an airtight container until needed. (Any leftovers can be kept in the freezer for later use.)

For the brownie: pre-heat oven to 170°C.

Combine flour, baking powder and salt in a container and put to one side.

Gently melt dark chocolate and butter together in a bowl set over a pan of simmering water. Whisk the mixture until combined and set aside to cool slightly.

Using an electric mixer, whisk eggs and both sugars together until the mixture is pale and thick; it should take 5–8 minutes. Add vanilla paste and then drizzle in the cooled chocolate mixture, beating until well combined. Fold the flour mixture in. Finally, fold the dark and milk chocolate chips through and then the hokey pokey.

Pour batter into six small individual frypans or two 20 cm pans and place in the oven for 20–30 minutes or until set. If making in the larger pans, cut into wedges. Serve immediately with a scoop of vanilla ice cream and an extra sprinkle of hokey pokey.

VARIATIONS

The first frypan brownie we did was Black Forest – add fresh or freeze-dried cherries to the mix and serve with cherry ripple ice cream. For an after-dinner version add peppermint flavouring and chopped marshmallows in the mix, which we served with a Vietnamese mint parfait. For our Violet Crumble variation we made a violet ice cream and topped with more hokey pokey... Then there is Red Velvet, with a swirl of cream cheese added before baking and a red velvet ice cream topped with red velvet crumbs. Our latest various is a Toastie/Coconut Rough version with coconut added to the brownie mix and served with coconut parfait and candied coconut.

"This frypan brownie always appears on our menu in some form... It's our all-time favourite!"

APRICOT & ALMOND FRANGIPANE PIE

Recipe by the team at **RANGIORA BAKERY**

SERVES: 6–8 | PREP TIME: 40 MINS, PLUS CHILLING & RESTING | COOK TIME: 45 MINS | SKILL LEVEL: 2 (MODERATE)

INGREDIENTS

Sweet butter pastry
120 g butter
70 g sugar
1 egg
a few drops almond essence
200 g flour
½ tsp baking powder

Almond frangipane
130 g butter, softened
130 g sugar
2 eggs
a few drops almond essence
130 g ground almonds
80 g flour, sifted
½ tsp baking powder

To assemble
¼ cup (80 g) apricot jam
canned or fresh apricots, halved
20 g sliced (flaked) almonds
100 g apricot jam
20 ml water

METHOD

For the pastry: mix the butter and sugar together until soft and combined. Lightly whisk the egg until yolk and white are mixed, then divide in two and set half aside to use in the filling. Add the other half of the egg and the vanilla to the butter/sugar mixture and stir in. Add the flour and baking powder and mix till smooth. Wrap the pastry and chill in the refrigerator for at least 1 hour, to harden up.

When the pastry is ready, roll it out to about 7 mm thick and use it to line a 25 cm tart mould. Chill for 30 minutes in the refrigerator.

For the filling: cream the butter and sugar together until pale. Lightly whisk the eggs with the half set aside earlier and add, a little at a time, to the butter/sugar mixture, beating until combined each time. With the last lot of egg, beat in the almond essence. Fold in the dry ingredients and mix until smooth.

Assembly and baking: Spread apricot jam over the base of the sweet pastry shell and cover with almond frangipane. Arrange apricot halves over the frangipane and sprinkle with sliced almonds. Chill in refrigerator for at least 15 minutes.

Pre-heat the oven to 190°C. Bake the pie for 45 minutes, until the centre of the pie is just firm. Leave to cool in the tin.

Heat apricot jam and water together in small saucepan until it comes to the boil. Strain. Brush over cooled pie and leave to set before serving.

TIPS

This is a delicious recipe that can be baked as a pie, a tartlet or even on a sheet tray. In this case I am using canned apricots, but plums, pears or any fruit can be substituted.

CREAMY RICE PUDDING

Recipe by **JULIE BIUSO** *from Shared Kitchen*

SERVINGS: 4–6 | PREP TIME: 20–30 MINS | SKILL LEVEL: 1 (EASY)

INGREDIENTS

250 g medium-grain rice
small piece of cinnamon stick
small piece of vanilla pod, split
3 strips orange zest
1 litre whole milk
75 g caster sugar
75 ml cream
1 tbsp orange blossom water

Garnish (optional)

pieces of vanilla pod
1 orange, peeled and segments cut out
ground cinnamon, for topping
sugar or vanilla sugar, for topping

GF

METHOD

Put rice in a saucepan, cover with cold water and bring to the boil, stirring often. Drain.

Put drained rice in a clean pan and add cinnamon stick, vanilla pod, orange zest and milk. Bring to a gentle boil, then immediately turn the heat down and simmer very gently for about 20 minutes, stirring often, until the rice is tender and the liquid has reduced by about a third; the pudding should be wonderfully creamy.

Remove cinnamon stick and vanilla pod and add sugar, cream and orange blossom water. Stir to combine and cook for a further few minutes until fully incorporated into the pudding. Spoon into bowls and serve warmish.

If you like, top bowls with vanilla pod and orange segments dusted with cinnamon and sprinkled with sugar, then glazed under a hot grill until the sugar caramelises.

TIPS

Keep the heat low and whip in enough cream at the end to give it a rich, creamy texture. Use whole milk, not fat-reduced, for best results.

You can brûlée orange segments under the grill for the top for added drama.

"I've loved rice pudding forever because it reminds me of my mum. This is fancier than hers, scented with orange blossom water and hints of cinnamon and vanilla."

RHUBARB & APPLE CRUMBLE

Recipe by **REX MORGAN** *from Boulcott Street Bistro*

SERVINGS: 4 | PREP TIME: 10 MINS | COOK TIME: 10–20 MINS | SKILL LEVEL: 1 (EASY)

INGREDIENTS

Fruit mixture

3 cooking apples
½ cup water
400 g fresh rhubarb
½ cup sugar
1 tsp orange zest, finely grated

Crumble

100 g butter, chopped
½ cup self-raising flour
½ cup soft brown sugar
½ cup rolled oats
icing sugar, for dusting

METHOD

Pre-heat the oven to 180°C.

Peel, quarter and core apples, then cut into slices 2 cm thick and place in a saucepan with water. Simmer for 5–8 minutes.

Meanwhile, wash rhubarb and chop into 1 cm lengths. Add rhubarb, sugar and orange zest to apple; return to the boil and simmer for 3 minutes.

Pour mixture into a greased shallow ovenproof dish or four small individual ones.

Make the crumble by rubbing butter into flour with your fingers, then mix in brown sugar and oats. Sprinkle crumble evenly over the fruit mixture.

Bake for approximately 20 minutes for a large dish and 10 minutes for small dishes. Dust with icing sugar and serve warm with vanilla ice cream.

TIPS

If you are using individual dishes, you may not need to bake for so long. Look for them to be turning golden brown and bubbling a little.

Rhubarb can be substituted with ripe stone fruit.

BREAD & BUTTER PUDDING WITH CRÈME ANGLAISE

Recipe by **TONY ASTLE** *from Antoine's*

SERVINGS: 6 | PREP TIME: 30 MINS | COOK TIME: 30 MINS | SKILL LEVEL: 2 (MODERATE)

INGREDIENTS

Pudding

1 loaf sandwich-sliced white bread, crusts removed
⅓ cup unsalted butter
⅓ cup Grand Marnier
1½ tbsp raisins
1½ tbsp mixed citrus peel
1½ tbsp apricot conserve
6 whole eggs
4 egg yolks
100 g sugar
2 cups milk
2 cups cream
brown sugar, for dusting
whipped cream, to serve

Crème anglaise

2 cups milk
1 vanilla pod, split open
6 egg yolks
75 g caster sugar

METHOD

For the pudding: cut bread to fit the bottom and sides of six individual large ramekins (9 cm across and 5–6 cm deep), and cut six rounds to act as tops. Butter all bread on one side and line the ramekins, butter side out.

Sprinkle bread lining with Grand Marnier. Place a portion of raisins, mixed peel and apricot conserve in each ramekin. Beat eggs, egg yolks, sugar, milk and cream with a whisk until thoroughly combined, then ladle custard mixture evenly into each ramekin, saving a little for topping up.

Leave to rest for 5 minutes, allowing the bread to soak up the custard. Pre-heat oven to 180°C.

Top up each ramekin with custard and place a bread lid on each, butter side up. Dust lids with brown sugar. Bake for 30 minutes or until custard is set.

For the crème anglaise: heat milk, add vanilla pod and leave to infuse for about 10 minutes. In a separate bowl, whisk egg yolks and sugar together. Bring heated milk up to the boil and pour onto the egg yolk mixture. Mix thoroughly.

Place combined egg yolk and milk mixture into a clean pan. Over a low heat, stir gently with a wooden spoon until the sauce thickens and coats the back of the spoon. Leave to cool, then pass through a sieve. Make sure you do not let this sauce boil, or it will curdle.

To serve: run a knife around the inside of the ramekins and carefully remove the bread puddings. Serve with crème anglaise and a quenelle of whipped cream. Garnish with a few strawberries if wished.

DEEP-DISH APPLE PIE

Recipe by **MARTIN BOSLEY**

SERVINGS: 8 | PREP TIME: 15 MINS, PLUS RESTING | COOK TIME: 1 HOUR | SKILL LEVEL: 1 (EASY)

INGREDIENTS

250 g plain flour
pinch of salt
80 g unsalted butter, cold
80 g beef lard, cold
ice-cold water
1.2 kg cooking apples
sugar, to taste
a little milk
caster sugar, for sprinkling
whipped cream

METHOD

Put flour in a mixing bowl with a good-sized pinch of salt. Cut butter and lard into chunks and rub into flour with your thumbs and forefingers. Add a little ice water to bring the mixture to a smooth but firm dough. Cover with a tea towel and rest in the fridge for 30 minutes.

Pre-heat the oven to 200°C. Peel, core and quarter apples, cutting them into thick chunks. You want them to retain some shape rather than turning to a purée as the pie cooks. Place apples in a pie dish and sprinkle with enough sugar to relieve some of their tartness – a rough guide is 1 tablespoon per apple. Toss the apples in the sugar.

Roll out pastry to fit the top of the pie dish. Wet the rim of the dish and lower pastry gently over the top of the apples, pressing the edge firmly to the rim of the dish. Crimp it with your thumb and forefinger or use the prongs of a fork. Cut away any excess pastry that may be hanging over the edge of the dish and use it to make a simple decoration for the top of the pie.

Cut two or three slits in the centre of the pastry to allow any steam to escape, brush with milk and sprinkle with caster sugar. Bake for 1 hour, until the pastry is crisp and golden, covering with tinfoil if necessary if it looks like it may burn.

You could serve custard with this but, for me, tradition dictates cream. Serve the pie hot and the cream will melt right through it.

APRICOT CRÈME BRÛLÉE

Recipe by **MICHAEL COUGHLIN** *from Olivers at the Victoria Store*

SERVINGS: 4 | PREP TIME: 20 MINS, PLUS COOLING
COOK TIME: 50 MINS, PLUS CHILLING | SKILL LEVEL: 2 (MODERATE)

INGREDIENTS

Apricot filling
100 g dried apricots
100 ml hot water
100 g caster sugar
150 ml orange juice
zest of 1 orange

Brûlée
500 ml cream
5 g vanilla paste
5 egg yolks
160 g caster sugar

GF

METHOD

For the filling slice apricots thinly and place in a pot with remaining filling ingredients. Bring to the boil, stirring constantly. Remove from the heat, cover and stand for approximately 2 hours, until apricots have softened and plumped up.

For the brûlée, place cream and vanilla in a medium-sized saucepan over a medium to high heat and bring to just below boiling point. Remove from heat, cover and sit for 15 minutes.

In a medium-sized bowl, whisk together egg yolks and 60 grams of sugar until well blended and just starting to lighten in colour. Add the vanilla and cream a little at a time, stirring constantly.

Pre-heat the oven to 150°C. Place a spoonful of soaked apricots into each of four 220 ml ramekins, then carefully ladle in the custard. Place ramekins in a large cake tin or roasting pan. Pour enough hot water into the pan to come halfway up the sides of the ramekins. Cover the tin/pan with tinfoil and bake until the custard is just set but still trembling in the centre – approximately 45–50 minutes. Remove ramekins from the tin/pan and refrigerate for at least 2 hours (up to 3 days).

To serve, place a dessertspoonful of the remaining caster sugar evenly on top of each custard. Using a blowtorch, melt sugar to form a crispy top. Allow crème brûlées to sit for at least 5 minutes before serving with 3–4 crisp pistachio biscotti (see page 94).

TIPS

The difficulty – and success – of this recipe lies in constant checking of the baking custard. Lower the temperature to 140°C on your first batch if you are unsure what will work for you, and never allow the heat to exceed 150°C.

"The inspiration for my crème brûlée comes from the intensely flavoured sun-dried apricots from the orchard across the river from where I used to live in Clyde."

BAKED VANILLA CHEESECAKE WITH STRAWBERRIES

Recipe by **KEVIN HOPGOOD** *from Hopgood's*

SERVINGS: 8 | PREP TIME: 10–15 MINS | COOK TIME: 1 HOUR 25 MINS, PLUS COOLING | SKILL LEVEL: 1 (EASY)

INGREDIENTS

Base

1 pack Digestive biscuits
35 g melted butter

Filling

1 vanilla bean
180 g sugar
500 g cream cheese, at room temperature
5 eggs
250 g cream
juice and zest of 1 lemon

Topping

50 g sour cream
20 g cream
15 g icing sugar

To serve

100 g sugar
100 ml water
300 g strawberries
a little caster or icing sugar
a squeeze of lemon juice

METHOD

Pre-heat the oven to 150°C. Line a 25 cm square baking tin with baking paper.

Place Digestive biscuits in a food processor and blend to a fine crumb. Drizzle in the melted butter and combine. Spoon biscuit mix into the base of the tin, spread it out evenly and press it down. Bake for 15 minutes or until golden. Set aside to cool.

Turn the oven down to 110°C. Split vanilla bean down the middle and scrape out seeds. Combine the seeds with all remaining filling ingredients and whisk thoroughly until smooth. Pour on top of the cooled base and bake for 60–70 minutes or until just set. The cheesecake should still be slightly wobbly when you take it out of the oven; you want the residual heat to finish the cooking to achieve the right texture. Leave the cheesecake to cool.

Whisk all topping ingredients together, then pour over cheesecake. Smooth it over, then place in the fridge to chill and thoroughly set.

Place sugar and water in a small saucepan and bring to the boil, stirring, until the sugar has dissolved. Cool. Slice 5 strawberries and brush with syrup, place on baking paper in a dehydrator and dry until crisp. (If you don't have a dehydrator, dust the slices with caster sugar instead.) Purée the remaining strawberries with sugar/icing sugar and lemon juice to taste.

To serve, carefully take the cheesecake out of the baking tin, cut slices with a hot knife and garnish with strawberry slices. Serve with purée (and extra strawberries, if wished).

BAKED APPLE CHEESECAKE TART

Recipe by the team at **COLENSO CAFÉ**

SERVINGS: 12 | PREP TIME: 40 MINS, INCLUDING CHILLING | COOK TIME: 50 MINS | SKILL LEVEL: 1 (EASY)

INGREDIENTS

Pastry
130 g butter
75 g sugar
1 egg
½ cup (80 g) self-raising flour
1¼ cups (150 g) plain flour

Filling
5 apples
zest of 1 lemon
½ cup (70 g) sultanas

Topping
175 g cream cheese
¼ cup (45 g) sugar
1 tsp vanilla essence
3 eggs
½ cup cream
1 tbsp cornflour

METHOD

Pre-heat the oven to 150°C fan-bake. For the pastry, cream butter and sugar together. Add egg and beat in, then mix in flours. Press into a 25 cm round springform tin and chill in the fridge for 20 minutes.

For the filling, slice apples thinly and arrange over the pastry, overlapping them onto each other. Sprinkle lemon zest and sultanas evenly over.

For the topping, soften cream cheese, add sugar, vanilla, eggs, cream and cornflour and whizz in a food processor until combined. Pour over apples. Bake for approximately 50 minutes, until a light golden-brown.

CHOCOLATE SELF-SAUCING PUDDING WITH PASSIONFRUIT POSSET

Recipe by **STEPHEN BARRY** *from Mount Bistro*

SERVINGS: 10 | PREP TIME: 20 MINS, PLUS CHILLING | COOK TIME: 15 OR 30 MINS | SKILL LEVEL: 1 (EASY)

INGREDIENTS

Passionfruit posset
500 ml cream
⅔ cup sugar
pulp of 8 passionfruit

Chocolate puddings
½ cup (100 g) sugar
2 tbsp Dutch cocoa powder
¾ cup gluten-free flour
1 tsp baking powder
pinch of salt
50 g butter
½ cup milk
½ tsp vanilla paste
1 cup boiling water

Topping
¼ cup brown sugar
2 tbsp white sugar
1 tbsp Dutch cocoa

GF

METHOD

For the passionfruit posset: put cream and sugar in a saucepan and bring to the boil, then simmer for 3 minutes.

Sieve the passionfruit pulp to remove the seeds. Add passionfruit juice to the hot cream and stir until well combined, then pour into small dishes and put in the fridge for a few hours, until set.

For the chocolate puddings: pre-heat oven to 180°C.

Sieve together all dry ingredients. In a separate bowl, melt butter and mix with milk and vanilla. Combine the dry with the wet ingredients and mix to a smooth batter. Put batter into a greased dish so it comes no more than a third of the way up the sides (use either deep individual muffin dishes or a single pudding bowl).

Mix together the topping ingredients and sprinkle on top. Just before it goes into the oven, carefully pour the boiling water over a spoon onto the mixture.

Bake for 15 minutes for individual puddings or 30 minutes for a single large one. The puddings are cooked once a skewer inserted into the centre comes out clean.

Serve puddings warm with a scoop of passionfruit posset on each plate.

TIPS

Feel free to substitute gluten-free flour with standard flour if gluten is not an issue for you. Remember to use deep moulds for the pudding as the mix can boil over and mess up your oven. A tray placed under the pudding can also catch any mix that may escape from the dish.

"I've tweaked this recipe a little bit and made it gluten- and egg-free because my daughter's allergic to both. This is a dessert she can actually have and enjoy, just as I did as a kid."

ROLY POLY PUDDING

Recipe by **PETA MATHIAS**

SERVINGS: 6 | PREP TIME: 15 MINS | COOK TIME: 30 MINS | SKILL LEVEL: 1 (EASY)

INGREDIENTS

225 g self-raising flour
1 tsp baking powder
½ tsp salt
110 g suet
150 ml water
300 g strawberry, raspberry, blackcurrant or plum jam
milk, for glazing
whipped cream, to serve

METHOD

Pre-heat the oven to 180°C.

Sift flour, baking powder and salt together, then mix suet in. Add water and quickly mix to a soft, wet dough.

Roll dough out roughly on a floured surface until it measures about 30 cm x 15 cm. Spread jam all over, but not quite to the edges. Dip a pastry brush in milk and brush the edges, then roll up loosely, starting at a short end.

Place on a greased baking sheet, brush with milk and bake for at least 30 minutes or until golden on top. Serve hot, sliced thickly, with whipped cream.

"The magic of recipes is that they connect you to the past. Roly poly pudding is an old-fashioned dish that my father used to make us kids. My mother was a plain cook and Dad had a sweet tooth, so we had dessert every night."

PANNA COTTA

Recipe by **LISA SCHOLZ** *from Saggio Di Vino*

SERVINGS: 4 | PREP TIME: 15 MINS | COOK TIME: 10 MINS, PLUS 2–3 HOURS TO SET | SKILL LEVEL: 1 (EASY)

INGREDIENTS

Panna cotta

3 gelatine leaves
500 ml cream
60 ml milk
1 vanilla pod, split lengthwise, seeds scraped out
25 g sugar
seasonal berries, for serving

Coulis

175 g sugar
175 ml water
splash crème de cassis or cherry liqueur
175 g raspberries

Passionfruit variation

2 gelatine leaves
150 ml freshly squeezed orange juice
3 passionfruit
25 g sugar

GF

METHOD

Soak gelatine leaves in a little cold water, until soft. Place cream, milk, vanilla pod and seeds and sugar into a pan and bring to a simmer. Remove the vanilla pod and discard.

Squeeze the water out of the gelatine leaves, then add them to the pan and remove from the heat. Stir until the gelatine has dissolved.***

Divide the mixture among four greased ramekins and leave to cool. Place in the fridge for at least an hour, preferably 2–3, until set.

For the coulis, place sugar, water and liqueur in a pan and bring to the boil. Reduce the heat and simmer until the sugar has dissolved. Take the pan off the heat and add the raspberries. Using a hand-blender, blend the sauce until smooth. Pass sauce through a sieve into a bowl.

To serve, turn each panna cotta out onto a serving plate. Spoon coulis over and serve with your favourite seasonal berries.

VARIATION WITH PASSIONFRUIT JELLY

*** Pour panna cotta mixture into a jug and allow to cool completely.

Soak gelatine leaves in a little cold water, until soft. Bring the orange juice, passionfruit and sugar to the boil and stir in squeezed-out gelatine leaves. Stir well to combine, cool slightly and strain through a sieve.

Divide the jelly equally between four ramekins and refrigerate until set (approximately 1 hour). Top up with the cooled panna cotta mix and refrigerate again for at least another hour, until set.

Serve as above.

TIPS

Panna cotta is very easy to make and you can use whatever fruits are in season. I prefer a traditional panna cotta with berries in summer. Do make sure you use fresh and best-quality ingredients; I think that's really important.

SUMMER BERRY TART

Recipe by **LAURAINE JACOBS**

SERVINGS: 6–8 | PREP TIME: 40 MINS, PLUS CHILLING | COOK TIME: 25 MINS | SKILL LEVEL: 2 (MODERATE)

INGREDIENTS

Shortcrust pastry
250 g plain flour
180 g butter
1 tbsp caster sugar
1 egg yolk
1 tbsp water

Filling
3 egg yolks
2 tbsp plain flour
2 tbsp cornflour
100 g caster sugar
2 drops vanilla essence
450 ml milk
2 egg whites

To assemble
2–3 punnets of berries – strawberries, raspberries, blackberries, blueberries or any other berries in season
icing sugar, for dusting

METHOD

For the shortcrust pastry: put the flour, butter and sugar in a food processor and pulse together to combine. Add the egg yolk and water and mix briefly until the mixture resembles fine crumbs. Turn out onto the bench and knead together to form a ball. Chill for about 20 minutes.

Pre-heat oven to 180°C.

Roll the pastry out on a lightly floured bench and use to line a 24 cm loose-bottomed flan tin. Line the pastry shell with tinfoil and fill it with rice or baking beans, so the sides do not slide down during cooking. Rest the pastry shell for at least 20 minutes in the refrigerator before baking for 25 minutes or until the pastry is golden.

For the filling: put the egg yolks, flour and cornflour and 1 tablespoon of the sugar together in a bowl. Add the vanilla and 2 tablespoons of the milk and whisk together until light and fluffy. Heat the remaining milk in a heavy saucepan until it reaches boiling point. Tip the hot milk into the egg yolk mixture and beat well. Return the mixture to the rinsed-out pan and bring to boiling point, stirring vigorously. The mixture should coat the back of a spoon when it's ready.

Tip this custard into a clean bowl, and chill – with the surface covered with plastic wrap to prevent a skin forming.

When cool, beat the egg whites with the remaining sugar to make a thick meringue and whisk this, little by little, into the custard. Keep the custard in the refrigerator until ready to serve.

To assemble: place the tart shell on a flat serving plate. Spread the chilled custard into the tart. Discard any stems or tops from the berries, pile the fruit onto the custard and dust lightly with icing sugar to finish.

TIPS

Top this tart with a variety of available berries for a superb effect. The tart shell is filled with delicious, sweet custard which is quite runny, so bake the crust ahead, prepare the custard and keep it chilled. Assemble the tart at the last moment.

"Berries have a short-lived season so I like to make the most of them. Pile on the fruit and enjoy this taste of summer!"

SWEET TAMARILLO & VANILLA PIE

Recipe by **SAM MANNERING** *from Homestead*

SERVINGS: 6–8 | PREP TIME: 25 MINS | COOK TIME: 20–25 MINS | SKILL LEVEL: I (EASY)

INGREDIENTS

500 g tamarillos, peeled
200 g brown sugar
1 egg, beaten lightly
zest and juice of 1 lemon
½ tsp vanilla paste or essence
500 g sweet shortcrust pastry
1 tbsp caster sugar

METHOD

Pre-heat the oven to 180°C. Take a pie tin or dish – I used a deep enamel plate 25 cm in diameter – and grease it with a little butter.

Chop the tamarillos up a little and let them sit in a bowl for several minutes, then drain them of most of their juice. You can drink the juice or save it for cocktail hour (it's damn good with gin, a little sugar syrup, a dash of bitters and topped up with some soda).

Combine the tamarillos with the brown sugar, egg, lemon zest and juice and the vanilla paste or essence, and mix well. Add a little more lemon zest if you think it needs it.

Roll out the pastry to a thickness of about 5 mm and use half to line the base of the tin, trimming the edges so that it hangs over the side by about 2 cm. Fill evenly with the tamarillo mixture, smoothing it on top. Use the remaining pastry to create a round lid. Place this on top, then seal the edges by pinching and folding the pastry all the way around.

Score the top lightly with a sharp knife, poke a few holes through the lid for steam to escape, and decorate the top with any remaining scraps of pastry as you see fit. Sprinkle a little caster sugar evenly over the top, then place in the oven and bake for 20–25 minutes, until the pastry is nice and golden-brown. Allow to cool a little, then serve – runny or whipped cream is an ideal bedfellow.

"I feel like we don't really do these American-style fruit pies very much down here. Give this one a whirl – it's dead simple."

CHOCOLATE SOUFFLÉ

Recipe by **BEN BAYLY**

SERVINGS: 4 (PLUS EXTRA BASE) | PREP TIME: 40–50 MINS | COOK TIME : 10 MINS) | SKILL LEVEL: 2 (MODERATE)

INGREDIENTS

Soufflé base

95 g butter

450 g good-quality dark chocolate

105 g egg yolk, at room temperature

Mould preparation

50 g butter

50 g sugar

Soufflé

150 g egg white

60 g sugar

150 g soufflé base

40 g white chocolate, chopped

20 g icing sugar

To serve

icing sugar, for dusting

fresh berries

GF

METHOD

Melt butter and chocolate together carefully. Fold egg yolks through. This will make about three batches of four soufflés.

To prepare the moulds, soften butter and use to grease four soufflé moulds, using a pastry brush. Place in the fridge and leave to set, then 'repaint' with the butter to create a nice thick layer. Be generous with the butter – you don't want the soufflés to stick! Pour sugar into the buttered moulds and roll the sugar around to coat all of the butter. As the soufflé cooks, the sugar will melt and combine with the butter to create a protective layer between the soufflé mould and the soufflé mix and stop it sticking to the sides of the mould.

Pre-heat the oven to 180°C. Have two bowls ready. Place egg whites in one bowl with 5 grams of sugar. While whisking continuously, slowly add the rest of the sugar, then whisk until you have soft peaks.

In the other bowl put the soufflé base. Give it a good mix to soften it a little, add white chocolate, then add one-third of the egg whites and mix. Carefully add the other two-thirds of the whites and fold in carefully. Spoon into your prepared soufflé moulds and bake for 10 minutes.

The soufflés will rise nice and high! Serve immediately with a dusting of icing sugar and some fresh berries.

LEMON TART

Recipe by **JIM BYARS** *from The Friday Shop*

SERVINGS: 6–8 | PREP TIME: 25 MINS, PLUS PASTRY | COOK TIME: 1½ HOURS | SKILL LEVEL: 2 (MODERATE)

INGREDIENTS

400 g sweet pastry
125 g icing sugar
125 g lemon juice
250 g eggs
175 g cream
icing sugar, for dusting

METHOD

Line a 20 cm flan ring tin with pastry, leaving a good overlapping edge. Rest for 15 minutes in the fridge. Pre-heat the oven to 200°C (or 165–180°C fan-bake). Line the pastry with greaseproof paper and weigh it down with baking beans. Bake for 20 minutes, then remove paper and beans and bake for another 5–10 minutes, until golden-brown. Turn oven down to 100°C.

Mix together icing sugar, lemon juice, eggs and cream until smooth. Fill the flan base and bake until set (approximately 60 minutes). Allow to cool, then remove from the ring tin and dust with icing sugar.

STEAMED DATE PUDDING WITH HOMEMADE VANILLA CUSTARD

Recipe by **JULIE BIUSO** *from Shared Kitchen*

SERVINGS: 6+ | PREP TIME: 50 MINS | COOK TIME: 1½ HOURS | SKILL LEVEL: 1–2 (EASY–MODERATE)

INGREDIENTS

Date pudding

butter, for greasing
120 g self-raising flour
pinch of salt
½ tsp mixed spice
90 g unsalted butter
30 g fresh white breadcrumbs
3 tbsp soft brown sugar
170 g fresh dates, pitted and chopped
1 lemon, grated finely
2 medium-sized (size 6) free-range eggs
1 tbsp golden syrup
2 tbsp milk

Custard

300 ml whole milk
½ vanilla pod
3 medium-sized (size 6) free-range egg yolks, at room temperature
1 level tsp arrowroot
2 tbsp caster sugar
extra caster sugar, for sprinkling (optional)

METHOD

Before starting, ensure that butter, eggs and milk are at room temperature.

Grease a 5-cup (1¼-litre) china pudding basin with butter. Prepare a paper covering by folding a large piece of greaseproof paper in half and making a 2 cm pleat at the folded edge. Open paper out and grease it with butter, then fold pleat back in, with the rest of the paper lying open like a book.

Sift flour, salt and mixed spice into a bowl. Roughly chop butter and rub into dry ingredients with two round-bladed knives or a pastry blender, then stir in breadcrumbs, sugar, dates and lemon zest.

Whisk eggs with golden syrup and milk, then tip into the other ingredients. Mix with a wooden spoon until smooth.

Turn mixture into buttered basin, then cover with paper, butter-side down, and tie securely with string. Transfer pudding to a large, deep (rather than wide) saucepan, putting a trivet or a small, clean cloth under the basin to stop it clattering during cooking. Fill pan with hot water to come about one-third of the way up the basin, and cover with a tight-fitting lid. Bring water to the boil, then turn heat to the lowest setting and gently steam pudding the for 1½ hours. Top up with boiling water from a kettle if water runs low.

When ready, remove pudding basin from pan, snip off string and remove paper. Cover basin with a serving plate, invert and leave for 10 minutes to drop, then remove basin.

For the custard, put milk in a small saucepan. Scrape in seeds from vanilla pod and add the pod, too. Heat gently until warm (not hot), then remove from heat and leave to infuse for 10 minutes.

Beat egg yolks, arrowroot and sugar together in a small bowl with a wooden spoon for 2–3 minutes until creamy and smooth. Blend in vanilla milk. Clean the saucepan, then return mixture to pan over a low-to-medium heat. Stir constantly with a wooden spoon until custard thickens and coats the back of the spoon. On no account let it reach boiling point, or it will curdle.

Remove vanilla pod (it can be washed, dried and reused later), then pour custard into a bowl. Serve hot, or sprinkle with caster sugar and cool, then cover and refrigerate.

"This is an old-fashioned dessert that takes me straight back to my mum's kitchen. Her steamed puddings were legendary."

SAFFRON CRÈME CARAMEL

Recipe by **MARTIN BOSLEY**

SERVINGS: 4 | PREP TIME: 30 MINS, PLUS CHILLING | COOK TIME: 30–40 MINS | SKILL LEVEL: 2 (MODERATE)

INGREDIENTS

Caramel

⅓ cup sugar
2 tbsp water

Custard

500 ml milk
pinch of saffron threads
60 g sugar
3 eggs
2 egg yolks

GF

METHOD

Grease four large cups or ramekins.

For the caramel: place sugar and water in a small saucepan; bring to a simmer and cook without stirring until it is a deep amber colour. Remove caramel from the heat, pour some into the bottom of each cup or ramekin and leave until set. This can be done two days in advance.

For the custard: place milk, saffron and sugar in a saucepan and bring to a lazy simmer, stirring to dissolve the sugar. Remove from the heat and allow to cool until warm. Whisk eggs and egg yolks together in a bowl, and, while stirring, pour the warm milk mixture over. Strain this mixture through a muslin or cheesecloth into a pouring jug. Ideally you should now refrigerate the mixture overnight to allow the flavours to develop.

When ready to cook, pre-heat oven to 165°C. Pour custard mixture into the prepared cups or ramekins and place them in a deep roasting dish. Half-fill the dish with warm water. Place the dish in the oven and bake for at least 30 minutes – the tops should barely tremble when gently shaken. Remove from the oven and refrigerate creams for at least 24 hours.

To serve, run a knife around the top edge of each mould and loosen the custard with the tips of your fingers. Invert onto a serving plate.

TIP

I like to remove the caramel left behind in the mould, break it up and serve it alongside the crème caramel.

TAMARILLO CLAFOUTIS

Recipe by **ANDREW & JULIA CLARKE** *from Victoria Street Bistro*

SERVINGS: 6 | PREP TIME: 15 MINS | COOK TIME : 20 MINS | SKILL LEVEL: 1 (EASY)

INGREDIENTS

50 g butter, melted
8 tamarillos

Clafoutis batter

50 g ground almonds
pinch of salt
1 tbsp plain flour
1 vanilla bean, seeds only
100 g caster sugar
2 eggs
3 egg yolks
250 ml cream
60 g sliced almonds
icing sugar, for dusting
150 g good-quality white chocolate, melted
ice cream

METHOD

Pre-heat the oven to 160°C. Brush six ramekins, about 10 cm in diameter and 4 cm deep, with melted butter. (Please note that the image opposite is a serving for two.)

Cut tamarillos in half and scoop flesh out in one piece with a spoon. Cut in half again and place in the bottom of the ramekins.

For the batter, mix together ground almonds, salt, flour, vanilla seeds and sugar. Add eggs and yolks, and mix well. Lastly, add cream and stir until combined.

Pour batter over fruit, filling to about 1 cm from the top of each ramekin, then sprinkle with sliced almonds. Bake for around 20 minutes, until golden and still slightly wobbly.

Serve hot from the oven with a good dusting of icing sugar, a drizzle of melted white chocolate and a big scoop of ice cream.

TIPS

This batter is easy to make in a food processor, but don't blend it too much once the cream is added as it can split.

Feijoas, poached rhubarb or fresh figs work really well as a substitute for tamarillos.

CHRISTMAS PUDDING

Recipe by **LAURAINE JACOBS**

SERVINGS: UP TO 12 | PREP TIME: 30 MINS | COOK TIME: 4½ HOURS | SKILL LEVEL: 2 (MODERATE)

INGREDIENTS

250 g raisins
250 g sultanas
250 g currants
250 g butter
250 g brown sugar
5 eggs
125 g plain flour
½ tsp ground cinnamon
½ tsp mixed spice
½ tsp salt
1 tsp baking powder
250 g soft white breadcrumbs
1 packet (150 g) glacé cherries, halved
zest of 1 orange, grated
½ tsp each of vanilla and lemon essence
4 tbsp brandy or rum

METHOD

Place the raisins, sultanas and currants together in a saucepan with just enough water to cover; boil for 1 minute. Drain and leave to cool.

Cream the butter and sugar together until light and fluffy. Add the eggs, one by one, beating well after each addition.

Sift the flour, spices, salt and baking powder together and add to the egg mixture with the breadcrumbs. Stir in the cooled mixed fruit, cherries, orange zest, essences and brandy/rum.

Pour into a greased 8-cup basin (or pudding steamer) and cover tightly with tinfoil. Place the basin into a large, deep saucepan. Add water to fill the saucepan at least halfway up the side of the basin, and bring to the boil. Reduce the heat to a simmer, and simmer for 4½ hours. Make sure that the water level doesn't drop too low, topping up with boiling water as necessary.

After 4½ hours, carefully remove the pudding basin from the saucepan. Leave to stand for 30 minutes to cool a little before turning out onto a plate.

Serve with warmed custard and ice cream.

"I remember my mother filling her Christmas pudding with silver coins. Back then I ate it because I wanted to find the money, but over time I grew to appreciate its almost feather-light qualities."

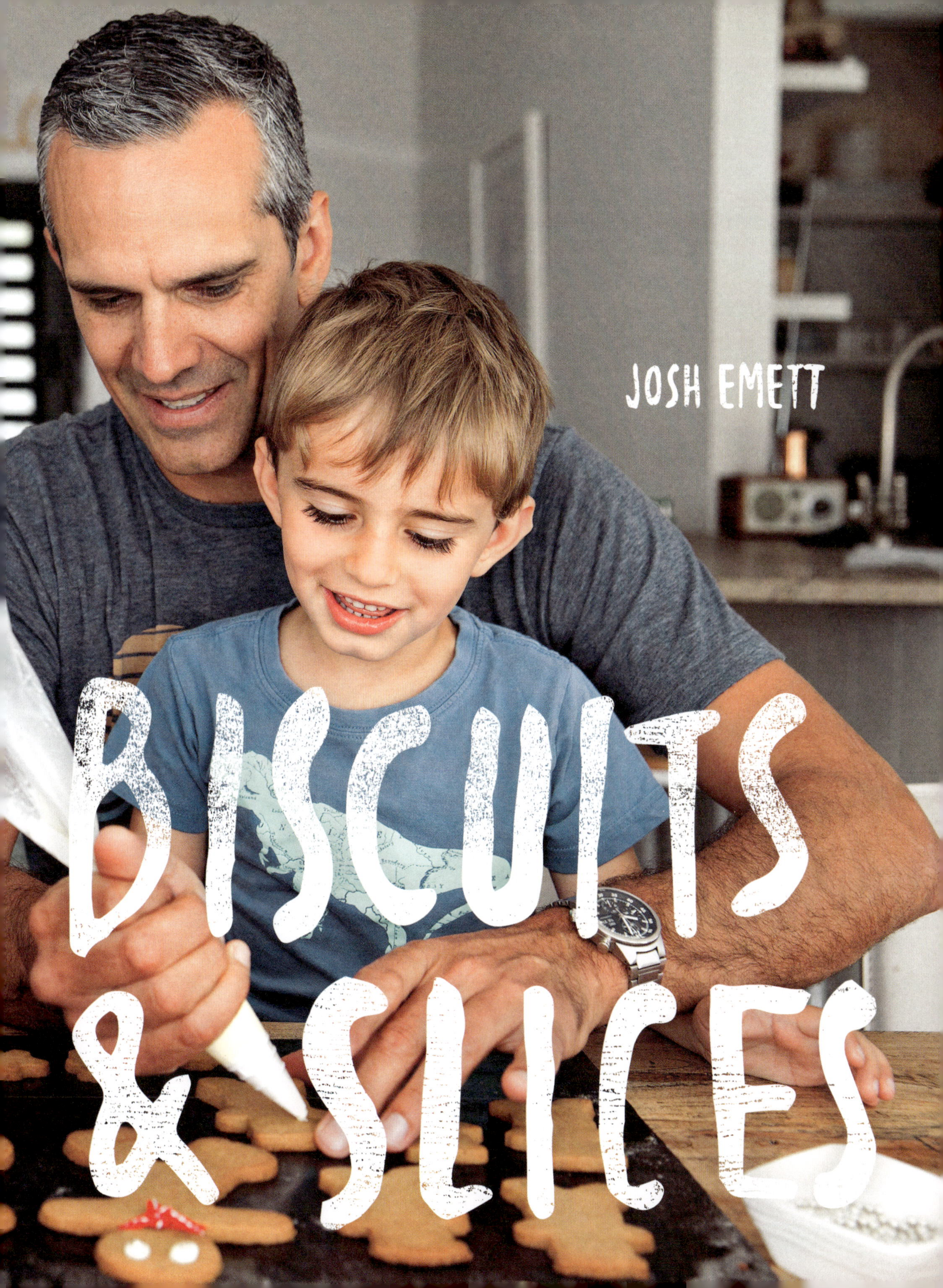
JOSH EMETT
BISCUITS
& SLICES

GINGERBREAD MEN

Recipe by **JOSH EMETT**

MAKES: ABOUT 12 | PREP TIME: 20 MINS, PLUS CHILLING | COOK TIME: 10 MINS | SKILL LEVEL: 1 (EASY)

INGREDIENTS

115 g soft brown sugar
115 g butter
2 tsp ginger powder
1 tsp cinnamon powder
1 thumb-sized stem ginger, finely grated
zest of 1 orange
30 g golden syrup
200 g plain flour

To decorate
pre-made vanilla frosting
red ribbon

METHOD

Pre-heat oven to 180°C.

Place all ingredients except flour in a mixer or food processor and whisk or blend until they are all creamed together.

Add flour and combine, then remove dough and roll into a disc. Wrap and place in the fridge to rest and chill for 20 minutes.

Remove from the fridge and cut into quarters, then roll each quarter out on a lightly floured surface, to a thickness of about 5 mm. Use gingerbread man cutters to cut out the shapes, placing them on greased/lined baking trays. Re-roll the leftover dough and repeat until all the dough is used.

Bake for about 10 minutes, then rest on the side on the trays until cool.

Put vanilla frosting in a piping bag with a 1 mm opening. Pipe faces and clothing on the men and then tie with red ribbon.

LEMON & RASPBERRY CURD KRUMMELTORTE SLICE

Recipe by **SOPHIE GRAY** *from Destitute Gourmet*

MAKES: 20 SLICES | PREP TIME: 25 MINS | COOK TIME: 25–30 MINS | SKILL LEVEL: 1 (EASY)

INGREDIENTS

Filling

2 cups (200 g) frozen raspberries

½ cup cheap raspberry jam

1 tbsp lemon juice

1 tbsp arrowroot mixed with 1 tbsp cold water

Crust

2 cups self-raising flour

1 cup sugar

zest of 1 medium-sized lemon

100 g butter

2 eggs

METHOD

Pre-heat oven to 180°C. Grease a 23 cm x 33 cm slice tin, then line with baking paper.

Place berries, jam and lemon juice in a small saucepan and heat gently. When berries are completely soft and the jam becomes liquid (about 5 minutes) stir arrowroot in and heat gently until mixture begins to thicken. Remove from the heat.

Place flour, sugar, lemon zest and butter in a food processor and pulse to combine. Add eggs and pulse to form crumbs. Pour three-quarters of the mixture into the prepared tin and press in firmly. Roll a rolling pin or a can from your pantry over the mixture to compress it evenly.

Pour berry mixture over the base evenly, then sprinkle on the remaining quarter of dough. Bake for 25–30 minutes, until golden. Cool in the tin, then gently lift out and slice.

VARIATIONS

Rhubarb, raspberry and orange: roast 350–400 grams of trimmed rhubarb stalks in the juice of ½–1 fresh orange at 190°C, for 15 minutes or until tender. Add the zest of 1 orange to the dough and fill the slice with the rhubarb and a handful or two of frozen raspberries.

Lemon or lime curd: add a teaspoon of vanilla essence to the dough, fill the slice with 1 generous cup of lemon or lime curd, and top with remaining dough.

Plum and ginger – or feijoa and ginger, or pear and ginger: add 1 teaspoon of ground ginger to the dough and fill with drained Black Doris plums, pears or feijoas, and top with remaining dough.

"This is one of my favourite slices, mostly because it's so easy to make, but it also looks really pretty – and I am deeply attracted to pretty food!"

AFGHAN YOYOS

Recipe by **SHAUN CLOUSTON** *from Logan Brown*

MAKES: 12 | PREP TIME: 30 MINS | COOK TIME: 12 MINS | SKILL LEVEL: 2 (MODERATE)

INGREDIENTS

Afghans

170 g butter
¼ cup coconut sugar
¼ cup sugar
1 cup plain flour
1 tbsp Dutch cocoa powder
1 cup cornflakes

Milk chocolate caramel

240 g milk chocolate
240 g sugar
240 ml cream
1 tsp salt
100 ml milk

To finish

¼ cup chopped walnuts (preferably New Zealand walnuts)

METHOD

Pre-heat oven to 160°C fan-bake or 180°C regular bake. Grease and line a baking tray.

Cream butter and sugars together until fluffy. Sift flour and cocoa together and add to creamed mixture. Lastly, stir cornflakes in. Place 24 heaped teaspoons of mixture on the tray and bake for 10–12 minutes. Cool on a wire rack.

Place chocolate in a medium-sized bowl. Heat sugar, without stirring, in a medium-to-large pot on a medium heat until it becomes a light golden caramel colour. Slowly pour cream in and whisk until smooth – be careful, as it can spit as you pour it in. Pour caramel over chocolate and whisk until smooth, then whisk salt and milk in. Set aside to cool.

Once everything is cooled, sandwich biscuits together with milk caramel and roll sides in chopped walnuts.

BRAN BISCUITS

Recipe by **TUI FLOWER**

MAKES: 20–30 | PREP TIME: 15 MINS | COOK TIME: 20 MINS | SKILL LEVEL: 1 (EASY)

INGREDIENTS

100 g butter
⅓ cup sugar
¼ cup milk
1¼ cups plain flour
3 tsp baking powder
1 cup bran

METHOD

Pre-heat the oven to 180°C. Lightly grease two oven trays.

Soften butter, add sugar and beat together well, until light and creamy. Stir in milk. (The mixture will not be smooth.) Mix flour, baking powder and bran in a bowl. Add to the butter mixture and stir to form a stiff dough.

Lightly flour a flat surface. Place about half the dough on it, cover with plastic wrap and roll out to about 3 mm thick. Remove plastic wrap and cut dough into rectangular pieces. Put the trimmings with the remaining dough and repeat rolling and cutting. Place biscuits on prepared trays.

Bake for about 20 minutes. Remove from trays to a cooling rack. When cold, store in an airtight container. Serve plain or buttered.

"Bran biscuits were a regular baking-day recipe of my youth. I think it was the rolling and cutting them out that I liked best – it is a process I still enjoy when baking."

STICKY LEMON SLICE

Recipe by **JULIE BIUSO** *from Shared Kitchen*

MAKES: ABOUT 28 SQUARES | PREP TIME: 15 MINS | COOK TIME: 45–50 MINS | SKILL LEVEL: 1 (EASY)

INGREDIENTS

Base

225 g unsalted butter, softened

70 g icing sugar

275 g plain flour

Topping

400 g granulated sugar

4 medium-sized (size 6) free-range eggs, beaten together

4 tbsp plain flour

1 tsp baking powder

zest of 2 lemons, finely grated

90 ml lemon juice, strained

icing sugar, for dusting

METHOD

Pre-heat the oven to 170°C. Line the bottom of a non-stick Swiss roll tin (32 cm x 21 cm) with baking paper.

Put butter in the bowl of a food processor and process until whipped, then add icing sugar and process until light in colour (creamed). Sprinkle flour over and process until the mixture starts to form a ball. Tip into prepared tin and press flat. If the mixture is sticky, keep your fingers dusted with plain flour. Bake base for 15 minutes, then remove from the oven and leave to cool in the tin.

While the base is cooling, make the topping. Tip sugar into the bowl of the food processor and pour egg in. Process for 1 minute. Transfer the mixture to a bowl, then sprinkle flour and baking powder over, and add the lemon zest and juice. Mix together with a large spoon.

Pour mixture on top of the base (it will fill the tin), then return to the oven and bake for a further 30–35 minutes, or until golden in colour and firmish to the touch. Cool in the tin, then dust with icing sugar and cut into squares. Transfer to an airtight container when cool.

"This super-delectable sweet-but-tart slice goes to show that a great recipe never dies – it tastes just as good now as when I first made it, back in 1985!"

PASSIONFRUIT MELTING MOMENTS

Recipe by **HESTER GUY** *from HG Catering*

MAKES: ABOUT 25 | PREP TIME: 20 MINS | COOK TIME: 15 MINS, PLUS COOLING | SKILL LEVEL: 1 (EASY)

INGREDIENTS

250 g butter, softened
1 tsp vanilla extract
80 g soft icing sugar
250 g plain flour
75 g cornflour
4 passionfruit

Butter cream

100 g butter, softened
110 g soft icing sugar

METHOD

Pre-heat the oven to 150°C (140°C if fan-baked). Line three baking trays with baking paper.

Beat butter, vanilla and sifted icing sugar with an electric mixer until pale. Stir in the combined sifted flours in two batches. Remove pulp from passionfruit – reserve 1 tablespoon of pulp for the butter cream and stir the rest into the mixture.

With lightly floured hands, roll the equivalent of 2 level teaspoons of mixture into balls and place about 3 cm apart on baking trays. Dip a fork into a little extra flour and press biscuits lightly.

Bake for about 15 minutes or until biscuits are a pale straw colour (the secret is to cook the biscuits in a slow oven so they barely colour). Stand biscuits on the trays for 5 minutes, then transfer to wire racks to cool.

To make the butter cream, beat butter and sifted icing sugar in a small bowl with an electric mixer, until pale and fluffy. Beat in reserved passionfruit pulp. Sandwich biscuits together with a teaspoon of passionfruit butter cream. Dust with a little extra sifted icing sugar, if desired. Store, well covered, in the fridge.

THE RICHIE McCAW SLICE

Recipe by **LYNN COLBERT** *from Ripe Delicatessen*

MAKES: 20 | PREP TIME: 25 MINS | COOK TIME: 40–50 MINS | SKILL LEVEL: 2 (MODERATE)

INGREDIENTS

300 g butter, diced
300 g chocolate buttons
6 free-range eggs
2 cups (440 g) caster sugar
1 tsp vanilla extract
1¼ cups (190 g) plain flour
1 cup (100 g) cocoa powder
1¼ cups (200 g) white chocolate
1 tbsp rice bran oil
1½ cups (300 g) cream cheese, softened

METHOD

Pre-heat the oven to 170°C. Grease a 20 cm x 30 cm high-sided slice tin and line with baking paper.

Melt the butter and chocolate buttons together in a heatproof bowl placed over a saucepan of simmering water. Alternatively, use your microwave – melt the butter and chocolate together on high in short bursts of 20 seconds, for 1 minute or until just melted, checking after each burst. Stir until combined and set aside to cool a little.

In a large mixing bowl, use an electric beater to whisk the eggs, sugar and vanilla together until thick and creamy.

Sift the flour and cocoa over the egg mixture. Using a large metal spoon, stir until smooth and glossy. Add the chocolate mixture and stir through until it is just combined.

Using either of the methods listed above, melt the white chocolate and oil together, stirring after each burst if using the microwave. Add the cream cheese and beat with an electric beater until well combined and smooth.

Pour half of the chocolate brownie mixture into the slice tin. Dollop spoonfuls of the cream cheese mixture on top. Carefully spread the cream cheese out until it covers the brownie mixture. Pour the remaining brownie mixture over the top, spreading it out so it covers the cream cheese mixture.

Bake for 40–50 minutes, or until just starting to set in the middle and a crust has formed. Remove from the oven and allow to cool in the tin for at least an hour before cutting.

"The Richie McCaw slice is named after our favourite All Blacks captain because it's as amazing (and delicious) as he is!"

CARAMEL OAT SLICE

Recipe by **JO SEAGAR**

MAKES: 16–20 | PREP TIME: 12 MINS | COOK TIME: 30 MINS | SKILL LEVEL: 1 (EASY)

INGREDIENTS

Base
2 cups plain flour
1 cup self-raising flour
1 cup desiccated coconut
2 cups brown sugar
3 cups rolled oats
2 eggs
300 g butter, melted

Filling
200 g butter
400 g sweetened condensed milk
4 tbsp golden syrup
1 tsp vanilla essence
dark and white chocolate melts (optional)

METHOD

Pre-heat the oven to 180°C. Grease a large 25 cm x 35 cm slice or sponge roll tin and line with baking paper. Make sure the paper has a good over-hang.

For the base, combine dry ingredients in a bowl. Add eggs and butter. Mix well, then press two-thirds of the mixture into the prepared tin.

For the filling, slowly melt butter, condensed milk and golden syrup together. Mix well, then add vanilla essence. Pour onto the base. Sprinkle the remaining crumbly mixture on top of the filling and bake for 30 minutes. Cool and refrigerate.

TIPS

Best to cut the next day, to get beautiful slices. Can be drizzled with melted dark and white chocolate to decorate.

CHOCOLATE CHIPPIE BISCUITS

Recipe by **SIMON HOLST**

MAKES: 12 LARGE BISCUITS | PREP TIME: 10 MINS | COOK TIME: 10–12 MINS | SKILL LEVEL: 1 (EASY)

INGREDIENTS

75 g butter
½ cup brown sugar
½ cup white sugar
1 large egg
½ cup chocolate chips
½ tsp baking soda
1¼ cups plain flour

METHOD

Pre-heat oven to 180°C (170°C fan bake). Line an oven tray with baking paper or a non-stick liner.

Microwave butter in a microwave-proof bowl for 1 minute. Add sugars and egg, and beat with a fork until mixed thoroughly.

Sprinkle chocolate chips into the bowl. Measure baking soda and flour into a sieve placed over the bowl; shake them into the bowl and mix everything together well.

Divide half the mixture into 12 walnut-sized balls. Place these on the tray, leaving room for spreading, and gently flatten to about 1 cm thick. (The mixture firms up a little on standing – if it is too soft to form into balls initially, you can just spoon it out onto the tray.)

Bake just below the middle of the oven for 10–12 minutes or until golden-brown – a fan oven is likely to cook the biscuits more quickly than a regular one. While biscuits are warm, lift them onto a cooling rack, then shape and cook the rest of the mixture the same way.

When biscuits are cold, store in an airtight container/jar.

"These are enormously popular and are great for snacking or inclusion in lunch boxes."

GINGER PISTACHIO CRUNCH

Recipe by **MICHELLE PATTISON**

MAKES: 24 SLICES | PREP TIME: 15 MINS | COOK TIME: 20–25 MINS | SKILL LEVEL: 1 (EASY)

INGREDIENTS

Base

300 g butter, at room temperature
1¼ cups (250 g) sugar
3 cups (450 g) plain flour
4 tsp ground ginger
2 tsp baking powder
¼ cup (50 g) crystallised ginger, chopped finely

Icing

240 g butter
4 tbsp golden syrup
3 cups (450 g) icing sugar
3 tbsp ground ginger
½ cup (60 g) pistachios, toasted

METHOD

Pre-heat the oven to 180°C. Grease a 25 cm x 30 cm tin and line with baking paper.

Place the pistachios in a baking tin and roast for around 5 minutes or until golden. Cool and chop roughly.

For the base, cream butter and sugar together in an electric mixer until thick and pale. Sift in flour, ginger and baking powder, and stir to combine. Fold in crystallised ginger. Press this mixture into the prepared tin. Bake for 20–25 minutes or until golden and cooked.

For the icing, in a small saucepan over a medium heat melt butter and golden syrup, stirring until combined, then remove from heat. Sieve icing sugar and ginger into a medium-sized bowl. Pour the butter mixture into the bowl and stir to combine.

While base is still warm, pour icing over it, using a spatula to spread the icing consistently. Sprinkle pistachios over the top. Allow to cool completely in the tin, then remove and cut into 24 slices.

"When kids come to my house I love to give them a stool to stand on in my kitchen so we can bake together, just like I used to do with my gran."

PISTACHIO BISCOTTI

Recipe by **MICHAEL COUGHLIN** *from Olivers at the Victoria Store*

MAKES: 24 | PREP TIME: 20 MINS | COOK TIME: 50 MINS | SKILL LEVEL: 1 (EASY)

INGREDIENTS

125 g egg whites
pinch of salt
125 g caster sugar
125 g plain flour
125 g pistachio nuts
5 g vanilla paste

DF

METHOD

Pre-heat the oven to 175°C. Line a loaf tin with non-stick baking paper.

In a large bowl and using an electric mixer, beat egg whites with salt until they just form stiff peaks. Gradually beat in sugar, beating until meringue mixture forms stiff, glossy peaks. Sift flour over mixture and fold in with nuts and vanilla, gently but thoroughly.

Spoon meringue mixture into loaf tin, smoothing the top, and bake in middle of oven until golden, 25–30 minutes. Cool loaf in tin on a rack for 15 minutes, then turn out onto rack to cool completely.

Reduce oven temperature to 150°C. Peel baking paper off and use a serrated knife to cut loaf crosswise into slices 3 mm thick. Arrange slices about 1 cm apart on two baking sheets and bake for about 20 minutes or until pale golden and crisp, switching position of the sheets halfway through. Cool biscuits on sheets placed on racks.

Biscuits keep in an airtight container at a cool room temperature for up to 10 days.

LOUISE CAKE

Recipe by **NATALIE OLDFIELD**

SERVINGS: 16 | COOK TIME: 20–25 MINS | SKILL LEVEL: 1 (EASY)

INGREDIENTS

Cake
150 g butter, softened
¼ cup white sugar
2 egg yolks
2 cups self-raising flour
¾ cup raspberry jam

Meringue
2 egg whites
½ cup sugar
1½ cups coconut

METHOD

Pre-heat the oven to 180°C. Grease and line a 30 cm x 20 cm slice tin.

Cream butter and sugar together until light and fluffy, then add egg yolks and beat well. Sift flour and stir in, then use your hands to achieve an even consistency.

Press mixture into slice tin, then spread jam over the top.

To make the meringue, beat egg whites and sugar until thick, then fold in coconut. Spread the meringue on top of the jam and cake.

Bake for 20–25 minutes. Cool in the tin before slicing.

TIPS

Don't be afraid to get your hands into this when preparing the base!

When spreading the meringue over the top, you can use a hot knife to help.

"This is a long-time favourite of many in my family. Most weeks, Gran would make this and share it with her loved ones."

FLORENTINES

Recipe by **ANNABELLE WHITE**

MAKES: 22 | PREP TIME: 40 MINS | COOK TIME: 20–25 MINS | SKILL LEVEL: 1 (EASY)

INGREDIENTS

70 g butter
75 g sugar (about ⅓ cup)
1½ tbsp crème fraîche
25 g mixed peel
50 g currants or sultanas
110 g sliced almonds
10 glacé cherries
1 cup chocolate buttons

GF

METHOD

Spray silicone muffin pans (7 cm wide) with oil and heat the oven to 180°C.

Melt butter in a medium-sized pot, add sugar and stir in. Once this is dissolved, add the rest of the ingredients except the glacé cherries and chocolate. With your beloved wooden spoon, stir well for a few minutes to make sure all the ingredients are well coated with the butter and sugar mix.

Remove from the heat and use a dessertspoon to divide the mix between the muffin pans. (About 1 heaped dessertspoon per pan will work.) Rip cherries into thirds and place on top of mixture. Let it cool slightly, and then push it down with clean hands to ensure an even spread all around the muffin pans. Bake for 20–25 minutes, or until a good golden brown. Cool completely in the pans.

Once florentines are cool, melt chocolate in a stainless-steel bowl set over a saucepan of simmering water (make sure the bowl is not touching the water). Place a spoonful of chocolate in the centre of each florentine and smooth it out using the back of the spoon in a circular motion.

Cool until chocolate is set, and store in an airtight container in the fridge. If they soften slightly, they make a delicious, easy dessert with a scoop of vanilla ice cream.

TIPS

You really require silicone muffin pans for this recipe – it doesn't really work with conventional bakeware. On sale, recently a set cost me $9, so a good investment.

This recipe also requires scales – and a set of digital scales is a super investment for any baker.

"Secret confession – this is my favourite dessert option! Chewy fruit, golden goodness and a hint of chocolate."

GINGER KISSES

Recipe by **HELEN JACKSON** *from Foodlovers*

MAKES: 20 | PREP TIME: 25 MINS | COOK TIME: 12–15 MINS | SKILL LEVEL: 1 (EASY)

INGREDIENTS

200 g butter
¾ cup (185 g) sugar
1 tbsp golden syrup
2 eggs
1¼ cups (180 g) plain flour
½ cup (55 g) cornflour
1 tsp baking soda
1 tsp baking powder
2 tsp ground ginger
1 tsp ground cinnamon

Icing

1½ cups (225 g) icing sugar
2 tbsp butter, melted
zest of ½ lemon, grated finely
2 tsp lemon juice
a little boiling water

METHOD

Pre-heat the oven to 170°C. Lightly grease 1 or 2 baking trays or line with baking paper.

Beat butter, sugar and golden syrup together until pale and creamy, about 5 minutes. Add eggs, one at a time, beating well after each addition.

In a separate bowl, combine remaining dry ingredients. Fold into beaten mixture. Drop 40 dessertspoons of mixture onto the tray(s) and bake for 12–15 minutes until firm to the touch. Lift kisses from the tray and cool on a wire cake rack.

In a small bowl, mix together icing sugar, butter, lemon zest, juice and enough boiling water to form a spreadable icing. Sandwich cooled kisses together with icing.

"Ginger kisses take me back to my childhood as they were one of my nana's favourites."

ANZAC BISCUITS

Recipe by **ROBYN MARTIN**

MAKES: 28 | PREP TIME: 10 MINS | COOK TIME: 10–12 MINS | SKILL LEVEL: 1 (EASY)

INGREDIENTS

125 g butter
¼ cup golden syrup
½ tsp baking soda
1 tbsp hot water
½ cup plain flour
½ cup sugar
1 cup desiccated coconut
1 cup rolled oats

METHOD

Pre-heat the oven to 180°C.

Melt butter and golden syrup in a saucepan large enough to hold all the ingredients. Remove from the heat. Dissolve baking soda in hot water and mix into the melted ingredients. In a separate bowl mix flour, sugar, coconut and oats together until combined. Mix into the butter mixture until well combined.

Using a measuring tablespoon, take spoonfuls of the mixture and place on an oven tray lined with baking paper. Press with a fork to flatten – allow room for spreading.

Bake for 10–12 minutes or until golden. Leave on the oven tray to cool and firm up before moving to a cooling rack.

"These melt-in-the-pot Anzac biscuits are for all working mothers who like to have home baking in their tins but are short on time. They are quick and easy to make, with success assured."

SPECULAAS BISCUITS

Recipe by **MICHEL LOUWS** *from M&M Food & Drink*

MAKES: 1 BLOCK | PREP TIME: 15 MINS, PLUS CHILLING | COOK TIME: 40 MINS | SKILL LEVEL: 1 (EASY)

INGREDIENTS

Speculaas spice mix
8 tsp ground cinnamon
2 tsp ground nutmeg
2 tsp ground cloves
1 tsp ground white pepper
1 tsp ground ginger
1 tsp ground cardamom

Dough
125 g unsalted butter
400 g brown sugar (see note adjacent)
½ tsp baking powder
1½ tsp bicarbonate of soda
115 ml water
1 tsp speculaas spice mix (see above)
625 g white (pastry/cake) flour

Topping
1 egg
2 egg yolks
handful of blanched almonds (optional)

METHOD

Speculaas spice mix: combine this lot and store in a ziplock bag or airtight container. (Try adding some to a wintery game or pork stew, dust over your apple sauce or use some over a bowl of granola!)

Anyway, the dough: make it the night before, as a 12-hour rest improves the baking qualities. It can be shaped into the famous windmills (this is a rather thin cookie, though nice), but, for me, the best is speculaas 'brokken' – the same dough but rolled out quite thickly, then brushed with egg wash and baked at a moderate temperature for quite a long time so that it becomes dry, crunchy and crisp.

So, beat butter and sugar together until soft. In a separate bowl, mix baking powder and bicarbonate of soda with water and add to the butter/sugar mix.

Now stir the speculaas spice mix through the flour and stir this into the other mixture until combined. Roll into a log, cover in plastic wrap and chill overnight in the fridge.

Next day, take out of the fridge nice and early so it can get to a manageable temperature (say, kitchen temperature). Pre-heat oven to 175°C.

Roll out between two sheets of plastic wrap or baking paper to 1 cm thick and, say, 10 cm x 10 cm big, or the size of your baking tray – you decide.

Lightly beat egg with egg yolks and brush over dough. If you want to go fancy, press some blanched almonds into the dough all over the top. Bake until dry and crunchy, about 40 minutes, but as every oven is different keep an eye on it and lower the temperature if it looks like it is getting too dark before being cooked through.

Cool on a wire rack, then sit down, grab a cuppa and eat a whole block, scattering crumbs as you go!

NOTE

The sugar we use in Holland is 'basterdsuiker', which you cannot get outside Holland. It's a mix of fine caster sugar with a dark syrup to give a slightly moist, soft caramel like sugar. Try different sugars until you find the one you like best.

OAT COOKIES

Recipe by **GEOFF SCOTT** *from Vinnies*

MAKES: 18 | PREP TIME: 15 MINS | COOK TIME: 18–20 MINS | SKILL LEVEL: 1 (EASY)

INGREDIENTS

125 g melted butter
1 cup sugar
2 cups oats (milk oaties or porridge oats)
½ cup plain flour
1 egg, lightly beaten
1 tsp baking powder
1 tsp vanilla essence
½ tsp ground cinnamon

METHOD

Pre-heat oven to 180°C.

Line a baking tray with non-stick baking paper. In a bowl, mix all the ingredients together. Scoop out teaspoonfuls of mix, roll into balls and place on the baking tray.

Bake for 14 minutes and then transfer onto a wire rack to cool.

JAM DROPS

Recipe by **HELEN JACKSON** *from Foodlovers*

MAKES: 30 | PREP TIME: 15 MINS | COOK TIME: 20–25 MINS | SKILL LEVEL: 1 (EASY)

INGREDIENTS

175 g butter
¾ cup (185 g) icing sugar
1 tsp vanilla extract
1½ cups (180 g) plain flour
3 tbsp (55 g) cornflour
¼ cup jam

METHOD

Pre-heat oven to 170°C. Lightly grease a baking tray or line with baking paper.

Beat butter and icing sugar until pale and creamy (about 5 minutes). Add vanilla and then flours and mix well. Roll the mixture into small balls and place on the prepared tray, then press a hollow into the centre of each. Bake for 15–20 minutes.

Remove from oven and carefully spoon jam into the hollows, then return to the oven for 4 minutes. Cool on a wire rack and then store in an airtight container.

"Kids love these and they are a great as a lunch box treat."

ITALIAN ALMOND TEA CUSTARD SQUARE

Recipe by **LAURENT LOUDEAC** *from Hippopotamus*

MAKES: 1 SLAB | PREP TIME: 25 MINS, PLUS CHILLING | COOK TIME: 15 MINS | SKILL LEVEL: 1 (EASY)

INGREDIENTS

3 sheets ready-to-use frozen flaky puff pastry

Custard

500 ml full-fat milk

4 tbsp Italian almond tea leaves

130 g caster sugar

2 whole eggs

2 egg yolks

55 g plain flour, sifted

10 g custard powder

50 g butter, at fridge temperature

Icing

50 g butter, softened

2 cups icing sugar

1 tsp vanilla essence

a little whole milk

METHOD

Pre-heat the oven to 215°C.

To make the pastry base: cut the pastry sheets to be around 25% larger than the tin you plan to use. (I found that when I cut my pastry exactly to size it shrunk a whole heap, which is not ideal.) You might need to stick two sheets together to get the right length. Place the pastry (still half-frozen) on a dampened baking tray lined with baking paper (sprinkle a bit of water on with your fingers). Prick the sheets all over with a fork. Bake for 10 minutes, take out of the oven, flip the sheets over, return to the oven and bake for another 5 minutes, or until both sides are nice and golden. Leave the sheets to cool.

To make the custard: in a medium-sized saucepan, warm the milk over a medium heat until it just starts to boil. Put in the tea leaves and infuse for 10 minutes.

In a large bowl, beat together the sugar and eggs (both whole and yolks) until the mixture is very thick and pale. Sift in the flour and custard powder and beat until evenly incorporated.

Pour the warm milk into the egg and sugar mixture, while continuously beating on low. Beat until everything is evenly mixed. Return this mixture to the saucepan. Heat the custard on a medium-to-low heat, stirring continuously and making sure the bottom and corners of the pan are well scraped so it doesn't burn. Stir until the custard becomes nice and thick; it should take about 5 minutes. Take the custard off the heat and stir in the butter. Put into a bowl and cover with plastic wrap, making sure it touches the custard, to avoid a skin forming. Place in the fridge to cool.

To assemble: line the tin you are using with baking paper and place one of the pastry sheets on the bottom. Pour the custard over and spread evenly. Place the second sheet of pastry over the top. Place the custard square in the fridge to set for 1½ hours.

"As a boy in the small town of Isse in the Loire Valley, it was a special Sunday treat to have a custard square or 'mille feuille' from my local pâtisserie/boulangerie... but not every Sunday!"

NEENISH TARTS

Recipe by **DAVID GRIFFITHS** *from Mister D*

MAKES: 12 | PREP TIME: 50 MINS, PLUS CHILLING | COOK TIME: 15–20 MINS | SKILL LEVEL: 3 (CHALLENGING)

INGREDIENTS

Pastry

350 g soft unsalted butter
1 tsp vanilla paste
150 g icing sugar
4 egg yolks
500 g plain flour
50 ml cold water

Filling

75 g soft unsalted butter
100 g icing sugar
1 tsp vanilla paste
finely grated zest of 2 lemons
60 ml lemon juice
150 g sweetened condensed milk

Chocolate toppings

150 g good-quality white chocolate
1 tsp vanilla paste
75 g good-quality dark chocolate

METHOD

Pastry: place butter, vanilla and icing sugar in the bowl of an electric mixer and beat till pale in colour. Add egg yolks one at a time, beating after each addition. Fold in flour, adding water at this stage too; combine everything but do not over-work pastry. Wrap in plastic food wrap and refrigerate for 30 minutes.

Pre-heat oven to 175°C fan-bake (195°C regular bake) and lightly grease 12 regular-size tart moulds.

Roll pastry out between sheets of plastic food wrap to about ½ cm thick. Cut out 9 cm circles and use to line the tart moulds. Cover pastry with baking paper and weight it down with baking beans. Blind-bake till pastry is golden, around 15–20 minutes. Cool a little in the moulds, then remove and place on a rack to cool completely.

Filling: place butter and icing sugar in the bowl of an electric mixer and beat till pale. Add vanilla, zest and juice and mix in, then add condensed milk and beat for 2 minutes. Fill tart shells, smoothing off the tops.

Chocolate toppings: Melt white chocolate in a bowl in microwave on high for short bursts, stirring frequently, then stir in vanilla paste. Allow to cool to room temperature. Dip each tart in white chocolate to completely cover the top, then allow to set.

Melt dark chocolate, stirring frequently. Use the back of a teaspoon to coat just half of the tart with dark chocolate for that classic neenish tart look.

CHOCOLATE CHUNK OAT COOKIES

Recipe by **JO SEAGAR**

MAKES: 24 | PREP TIME: 10 MINS | COOK TIME: 15–20 MINS | SKILL LEVEL: 1 (EASY)

INGREDIENTS

250 g butter, softened
3 tbsp sweetened condensed milk
¾ cup sugar
1½ cups plain flour
1½ cups rolled oats
1 tsp baking powder
200 g dark chocolate, chopped roughly

METHOD

Pre-heat the oven to 180°C. Line two baking trays with baking paper.

Beat butter, condensed milk and sugar together, until light and creamy. Add flour, rolled oats, baking powder and chocolate chunks.

Flatten spoonfuls on the prepared trays and cook for 15–20 minutes until golden-brown. Cool on a wire rack and store in an airtight container.

TIP

To save having to chop the chocolate, use large chocolate buttons.

"This classic recipe is well-received at morning or afternoon tea – great for filling the tins and loved by all."

CHOCOLATE FUDGE SLICE

Recipe by the team at **COLENSO CAFÉ**

SERVINGS: 36 | PREP TIME: 15 MINS, PLUS COOLING | SKILL LEVEL: 1 (EASY)

INGREDIENTS

4 x 250 g packets Vanilla Wine biscuits

1 cup sultanas

500 g butter

2 cups sugar

2 tsp vanilla essence

1 cup good-quality cocoa powder

5 eggs, beaten lightly

METHOD

Crush biscuits in a food processor, or with a rolling pin, and place in a large bowl. Add sultanas and mix.

Dice butter and place in a medium-sized saucepan. Partially melt butter, then remove from the heat and add sugar, vanilla, cocoa and eggs. Stir until combined and butter is melted fully. Pour into crushed biscuits and mix well. Turn into a 24 cm square cake tin, press down firmly and leave to cool in the fridge. Cut into 36 squares. Store in the fridge in an airtight container – it makes enough to feed many!

TIPS

The chocolate should look smooth and glossy; do not overcook it.

CHOCOLATE PEPPERMINT SLICE

Recipe by the team at **RANGIORA BAKERY**

MAKES: 24 SLICES | PREP TIME: 20 MINS, PLUS COOLING/SETTING
COOK TIME: 25 MINS | SKILL LEVEL: 1 (EASY)

INGREDIENTS

Base

300 g butter, melted
380 g plain flour
1¼ tsp baking powder
130 g brown sugar
170 g desiccated coconut
25 g cocoa powder

Topping

85 g Kremelta or confectionery fat
600 g icing sugar
100 ml milk
½ tsp peppermint essence
2 drops green food colouring (optional)

Ganache

125 ml cream
65 g chocolate, chopped

METHOD

For the base: pre-heat oven to 185°C. Grease a 30 cm x 25 cm sponge-roll tin and line with baking paper.

In a large bowl, mix butter and dry ingredients until combined. Tip into tin and press into the base firmly. Bake for about 25 minutes, until firm in the middle. Cool in the tin.

For the topping: melt Kremelta or confectionery fat. Add remaining ingredients and slowly stir in until smooth. Smooth out topping over the cooled base and allow to set.

For the ganache: place cream in a small saucepan and warm to 90°C (just before boiling point). Remove from the heat, add chocolate and stir until smooth. Spread on top of slice and leave to cool completely. When cold, cut into bars.

Optional feathering: substitute chocolate with white chocolate in the ganache. Take a small amount of ganache out and add a drop of green colouring. Pour white chocolate ganache over topping, then straight away pipe on lines of green chocolate and use a knife backwards and forwards to pull the lines into feathers.

PEANUT BROWNIES

Recipe by **NATALIE OLDFIELD**

MAKES: ABOUT 24 | PREP TIME: 20–25 MINS | COOK TIME: 20–25 MINS | SKILL LEVEL: 1 (EASY)

INGREDIENTS

250 g butter, softened
2 cups sugar
2 eggs
2 tsp vanilla essence
2 cups plain flour
2 tbsp cocoa powder
½ tsp salt
1 tsp baking powder
2½ cups roasted peanuts
1 cup desiccated coconut

METHOD

Pre-heat the oven to 170°C. Grease and line a baking tray.

Cream butter and sugar together until light and fluffy. Add eggs one at a time, beating well after each addition, then add vanilla and combine. Sift in flour, cocoa, salt and baking powder. Fold to combine. Lastly, add roasted peanuts and coconut. Mix together well.

Roll mixture into tablespoon-sized balls and press to flatten slightly when placing on baking tray. Bake for 20–25 minutes. Cool on a rack.

TIP

To roast your own peanuts, put them in a baking dish in an oven pre-heated to 120°C for 20 minutes, shaking them occasionally. You can keep their skins on – they're not too husky for this recipe.

"My granny used to make a batch of these for us on our birthdays and present them to us in a beautiful biscuit tin. The smell of them baking is like nothing else!"

APPLE, CINNAMON & MAPLE SHORTCAKE

Recipe by **SAM MANNERING** *from Homestead*

MAKES: 10 SQUARES | PREP TIME: 25 MINS | COOK TIME: 30 MINS | SKILL LEVEL: 1 (EASY)

INGREDIENTS

2 large apples, cored and sliced thinly
zest and juice of 1 lemon
3 tbsp maple syrup
250 g butter
¾ cup brown sugar
1 egg
1 tsp vanilla essence
2½ cups plain flour
2 tsp baking powder
½ tsp ground cinnamon

METHOD

Pre-heat the oven to 180°C. Grease a shallow baking tin (approximately 35 cm x 25 cm) and line with baking paper.

Combine the sliced apple, lemon zest and juice and maple syrup.

In a large mixing bowl, beat together the butter and brown sugar until light and fluffy. Add the egg and vanilla and beat in well. Sift in the flour, baking powder and cinnamon and fold into the mixture until everything is combined. Press two-thirds of this mixture into the lined tin, then spread the apple mixture over the top, pouring any syrup over as well. Dot the remaining third of the mixture over the top, place in the oven and bake for about 30 minutes, until risen and golden. Allow to cool in the tin before cutting into squares and devouring.

"I've always been envious of my mother's innate ability to wing this sort of thing. Every time I ask her for anything resembling a precise recipe she is infuriatingly vague. Being a chef, I daren't improvise with baking, so this is my take on what she does. I bet she'll tell me it's 'passable'."

LEMON FUDGE SLICE

Recipe by **MICHELLE PATTISON**

MAKES: 18 SQUARES | PREP TIME: 15 MINS, PLUS COOLING | SKILL LEVEL: 1 (EASY)

INGREDIENTS

Base

2 packets (530 g) Wine biscuits

1 can (395 g) sweetened condensed milk

200 g butter, melted

¼ cup lemon juice

2 tbsp (35 g) glacé mixed peel

1 cup (90 g) long-thread desiccated coconut

Filling

45 g butter, melted

zest of 1 lemon

1 tbsp lemon juice

3½ cups (520 g) icing sugar

4 tbsp boiling water

METHOD

Grease a 20 cm x 30 cm tin and line with baking paper.

Using a food processor, blitz Wine biscuits into crumbs. In a large bowl pour the biscuit crumbs, condensed milk, melted butter, lemon juice, mixed peel and coconut, and stir until combined. Press firmly into the base of the tin.

For the filling, in a medium-sized bowl mix butter, lemon zest and juice, icing sugar and boiling water. Stir until combined into a smooth consistency, adding more water if required. Pour over the base, using a spatula to spread the icing consistently. Leave to cool completely, then slice 5 cm x 5 cm squares. Store in an airtight container in the refrigerator.

SHORTBREAD

Recipe by **ANNABELLE WHITE**

MAKES: 28–30 | PREP TIME: 40 MINS, INCLUDING CHILLING | COOK TIME: 15–20 MINS | SKILL LEVEL: 1 (EASY)

INGREDIENTS

300 g butter, softened slightly

1 cup icing sugar

3 cups plain flour

METHOD

Cream butter and sugar together. Mix in flour. Form the mixture into a long sausage shape (30 cm x 4.5 cm), cover in plastic wrap and place in the fridge for 20 minutes.

Pre-heat the oven to 160°C fan-bake or 180°C regular bake. Unwrap shortbread dough and cut into slices about 1 cm thick. Place on a lightly greased baking tray.

Prick with a fork and bake for 15–20 minutes. Make sure there is some colour on the shortbread for maximum flavour. Store in an airtight container. If for any reason air does get in and the shortbread softens, you can re-bake it for a few minutes to refresh it and make it firmer again.

TIPS

Placing the dough in the fridge is important. If pressed for time, you can freeze the dough at this stage and bake it off later.

"The rattling of the tins and the sight of these delicious accompaniments to a cup of tea restore flagging energies and cheer the soul."

BELGIUM BISCUITS

Recipe by **ROBYN MARTIN**

MAKES: 14 | PREP TIME: 25 MINS, PLUS COOLING | COOK TIME: 12–15 MINS | SKILL LEVEL: 1 (EASY)

INGREDIENTS

Biscuits

125 g butter
¼ cup brown sugar
1 egg
1¾ cups plain flour
1 tsp baking powder
1 tsp ground cinnamon
1 tsp ground ginger
1 tsp mixed spice
1 tsp cocoa powder
about ½ cup raspberry jam

Icing

1 cup icing sugar
2 drops pink food colouring
hot water

Coloured sugar

1 tbsp sugar
1 drop pink food colouring

METHOD

Pre-heat the oven to 180°C. Grease an oven tray or line with baking paper.

Melt butter in a saucepan large enough to hold all the ingredients. Remove from the heat and mix in sugar and egg, beating with a wooden spoon until well combined. Sift flour, baking powder, spices and cocoa into the saucepan and mix until combined.

Roll dough out between two sheets of baking paper to 3 mm thick. Using a 6 cm biscuit cutter, cut out rounds. Carefully lift the rounds and place on oven tray. Bring the dough scraps together and repeat the rolling and cutting. Bake for 12–15 minutes or until lightly golden, removing to a rack to cool.

Sift icing sugar into a bowl, then add food colouring and enough hot water to make a spreadable icing. Mix sugar and food colouring together in a separate small bowl.

When biscuits are cold, ice half of them and sprinkle with coloured sugar. Place 1 tablespoon of raspberry jam in the centre of the baking-tray side of the remaining biscuits. Top with an iced biscuit.

NATALIE OLDFIELD

CAKES & LOAVES

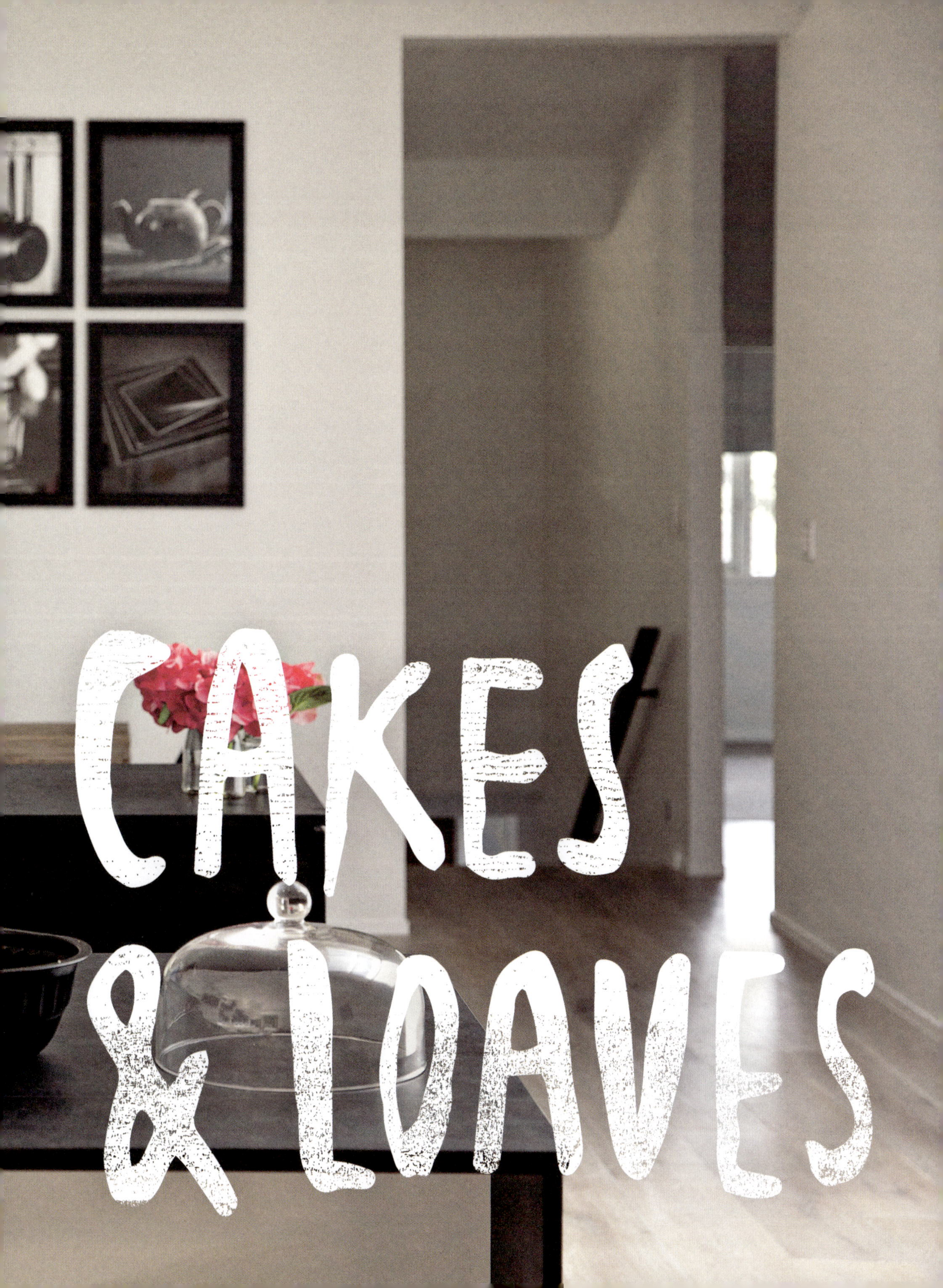

NEAPOLITAN CAKE

Recipe by **NATALIE OLDFIELD**

SERVINGS: 8 | PREP TIME: 25 MINS | COOK TIME: 50–60 MINS | SKILL LEVEL: 1 (EASY)

INGREDIENTS

Cake

220 g butter, softened
2¼ cups caster sugar
4 eggs
2 tsp vanilla essence
2 cups plain unsweetened yoghurt
3½ cups plain flour
1½ tsp baking powder
1½ tsp baking soda
2 tbsp cocoa powder, sifted
2 tbsp milk
2 tsp raspberry essence

Icing

2 cups icing sugar
4 tbsp blueberry juice

METHOD

For the cake: pre-heat oven to 180°C. Grease a 25 cm cake tin and line with baking paper, or grease a bundt tin with butter or cooking spray. Set aside.

Cream butter and sugar together until light and fluffy. Add eggs, one at a time, mixing well after each addition. Lastly, add vanilla and yoghurt and mix until just combined.

Sift flour, baking powder and baking soda together into a separate bowl. Add to creamed mixture and fold in until just combined.

Divide the mixture between three separate bowls. Fold sifted cocoa powder and milk into one portion, fold raspberry essence into another portion and leave the third portion plain.

Drop large spoonfuls of the mixtures into the prepared tin, alternating between the different colours. Bake for approximately 50–60 minutes.

When done (a skewer inserted into the middle comes out clean), leave in tin for 5–10 minutes and then turn out onto a wire rack to cool completely.

For the icing: sift icing sugar into a bowl and add blueberry juice, mixing to combine. The icing will be a little runny.

Once cake has cooled, pour icing on top and let it drizzle down the sides. Serve at room temperature, with cream if desired!

RED VELVET CUPCAKES

Recipe by **LAUREL WATSON** *from Petal*

MAKES: 20 | PREP TIME: 10 MINS | COOK TIME: 15 MINS | SKILL LEVEL: 1 (EASY)

INGREDIENTS

340 g caster sugar
300 g plain flour
1 tsp salt
1 tsp baking soda
12 g cocoa powder
230 g buttermilk
300 g canola oil
1 tbsp vinegar
1 tbsp good-quality vanilla essence
2 tbsp red food colouring
60 g water
2 eggs

METHOD

Pre-heat oven to 190°C. Line muffin tins with 20 cupcake papers.

Sift all dry ingredients together in one bowl and mix all wet ingredients together in another.

Place dry ingredients in the bowl of a stand mixer, then pour in wet ingredients. Mix on a slow speed to combine, then scrape down the bowl and mix again until just smooth.

Divide batter into cupcake papers. Bake for 15 minutes or until a skewer comes out clean from the centre of the cupcake.

Cool on a wire rack, then ice with flavoured cream cheese icing (see below).

CREAM CHEESE ICING

Recipe by **LAUREL WATSON** *from Petal*

MAKES: ENOUGH FOR 20 CUPCAKES | PREP TIME: 5 MINS | SKILL LEVEL: 1 (EASY)

INGREDIENTS

100 g butter, at room temperature
150 g cream cheese, at room temperature
3 cups icing sugar
pinch of salt
1 tsp Lorann flavour of your choice (see tip)

GF

METHOD

Blend butter and cream cheese in a bowl or food processor until smooth. Beat in icing sugar, salt and flavouring, adding a little icing sugar or water if necessary to achieve a spreadable consistency. Spread over cooled cupcakes.

TIP

The best essences we have found in New Zealand are the Lorann flavours. A little goes a long way so you can go wild with flavour combos without breaking the bank. Have some fun and mix it up!

LEMON CUPCAKES

Recipe by **LAUREL WATSON** *from Petal*

MAKES: 20 | PREP TIME: 10 MINS | COOK TIME: 15 MINS | SKILL LEVEL: 1 (EASY)

INGREDIENTS

340 g caster sugar
300 g plain flour
1 tsp salt
1 tsp baking soda
230 g lemon yoghurt
300 g canola oil
1 tbsp vinegar
1 tsp lemon essence
2 eggs

METHOD

Pre-heat oven to 190°C. Line muffin tins with 20 cupcake papers.

Sift all dry ingredients together in one bowl and mix all wet ingredients together in another.

Place dry ingredients in the bowl of a stand mixer and then pour in wet ingredients. Mix on a slow speed to combine, then scrape down the bowl and mix again until just smooth.

Divide batter into cupcake papers. Bake for 15 minutes or until a skewer comes out clean from the centre of the cupcake.

Cool on a wire rack, then ice with flavoured cream cheese icing (see page 134).

MANGO CUPCAKES

Recipe by **LAUREL WATSON** *from Petal*

MAKES: 20 | PREP TIME: 10 MINS | COOK TIME: 15 MINS | SKILL LEVEL: 1 (EASY)

INGREDIENTS

340 g caster sugar
320 g plain flour
1 tsp salt
1 tsp baking soda
115 g mango purée
115 g buttermilk
300 g canola oil
1 tbsp vinegar
2 eggs

METHOD

Pre-heat oven to 190°C. Line muffin tins with 20 cupcake papers.

Sift all dry ingredients together in one bowl and mix all wet ingredients together in another.

Place dry ingredients in the bowl of a stand mixer, then pour in wet ingredients. Mix on a slow speed to combine, then scrape down the bowl and mix again until just smooth.

Divide batter into cupcake papers. Bake for 15 minutes or until a skewer comes out clean from the centre of the cupcake.

Cool on a wire rack, then ice with flavoured cream cheese icing (see page 134).

PEACHES & CREAM SPONGE CAKE

Recipe by **DEAN BRETTSCHNEIDER**

SERVINGS: 6–8 | PREP TIME: 20 MINS | COOK TIME: 25–30 MINS | SKILL LEVEL: 2 (MODERATE)

INGREDIENTS

5 eggs, at room temperature
150 g caster sugar
160 g plain flour
5 g (1 tsp) baking powder
few drops vanilla extract (optional)
50 g butter, melted

To assemble

4 tbsp raspberry jam
500 ml fresh cream
few drops vanilla extract
1 can peaches, drained in a sieve
handful of fresh raspberries
a little icing sugar

METHOD

Pre-heat the oven to 190°C. Grease and flour a 20 cm round cake tin.

In an electric mixer and using the whisk attachment, whisk together eggs and sugar to the ribbon stage (this is when the mixture is thick, and when trailed on itself it will hold its own weight for about 10 seconds before sinking into the mixture).

Sieve flour and baking powder together and carefully fold through the egg/sugar foam mixture. Once flour is three-quarters folded through the foam, add melted butter and continue to fold through gently. Avoid over-mixing at this stage or you will lose all the precious air bubbles you have created.

Immediately place mixture in the prepared cake tin. Bake until sponge is set, approximately 25–30 minutes. Cool completely in the tin.

When cool, remove from the tin and cut horizontally into three equal-sized layers. Whip cream with sugar and vanilla until fairly firm. Spread raspberry jam on the first layer of sponge and spread a layer of whipped cream on top of that. Add some chopped pieces of peach, then place the next layer of sponge on top and press down lightly.

Spread another layer of whipped cream on the second layer of sponge, add some chopped pieces of peach and top with the final layer of sponge, pressing down lightly again.

Finally, spread remaining whipped cream on the top layer of sponge, leaving a clear ring about 1½ cm from the edge. Arrange thin slices of peach around the outside and add raspberries to the middle. Lightly sprinkle the raspberries with icing sugar.

"Sometimes there is nothing better than the simplicity of a vanilla sponge, but adding peaches and cream makes it just a little bit naughty!"

FARMHOUSE SULTANA CAKE

Recipe by **JO SEAGAR**

SERVES: 10–12 | PREP TIME: 20 MINS, PLUS COOLING | COOK TIME: 1½ HOURS | SKILL LEVEL: 1 (EASY)

INGREDIENTS

500 g sultanas
½ cup brandy, whisky or cold tea
250 g butter
1 cup sugar
5 eggs
1 tsp vanilla extract
2½ cups plain flour
1 tsp baking powder
¼ tsp salt

METHOD

Put sultanas in a saucepan, cover with cold water and bring to the boil. Simmer for 5 minutes, then drain. Place sultanas in a bowl and pour the brandy, whisky or tea over. Leave to cool.

Pre-heat oven to 160°C. Grease a 20 cm square cake tin and line with non-stick baking paper.

Cream butter and sugar together until light and fluffy. Add eggs, one at a time, beating well after each addition. Add sultana mixture and vanilla to the egg mixture and combine. Sift flour, baking powder and salt into the mixture and fold in.

Pour into tin and bake for 1½ hours, or until a skewer inserted in the middle of the cake comes out clean. Cool in the tin for 5 minutes, then turn out onto a wire rack to cool completely. Store in an airtight container.

"This is a very popular heritage recipe I updated from an old South Island sheep station cookhouse notebook. It would have been made to feed the shearers or musterers for smoko. The cake keeps really well, retains its moistness and even travels well in a stockman's saddlebag!"

GINGERBREAD

Recipe by **CAZNA GILDER** *from Mrs Clark's Cafe*

SERVINGS: 8 | PREP TIME: 15 MINS | COOK TIME: 45 MINS | SKILL LEVEL: 1 (EASY)

INGREDIENTS

50 g butter
1 tbsp each of molasses, treacle and golden syrup
2 eggs
1 cup yoghurt
1 cup milk
1 tsp vanilla essence
3 cups plain flour
2 tsp baking powder
1 tbsp ground ginger
1 tsp mixed spice
a good pinch of sea salt
½ cup brown sugar

METHOD

Pre-heat the oven to 165°C. Grease and line a loaf tin (23 cm x 13 cm x 7 cm deep).

Melt butter in a largish pan, then add molasses, treacle and golden syrup, and melt together. Add eggs, yoghurt, milk and vanilla. Beat together until smooth as.

Sift flour, baking powder, spices and salt together, then add sugar. Make a well in the centre of the dry ingredients and pour in all the wet mix – beat furiously until smooth and yummy. Resist eating the mix, and pour it into the loaf tin. Bake for 45 minutes, cool in the tin, then slice, eat and enjoy.

TIP

To make 'easy as' caramel sauce, put 1 cup brown sugar and 1 cup cream in a microwave-safe jug, heat on high for 2 minutes, stir, then heat for another 2 minutes. Cool to let it thicken up.

"This gingerbread is the ultimate in comfort food. I swear, even the staunchest ginger hater will be converted – I see it every day!"

FESTIVE CELEBRATION CAKE

Recipe by **NICI WICKES**

SERVES: 10–12 | PREP TIME: 30 MINS, PLUS CHILLING | COOK TIME: 40–45 MINS | SKILL LEVEL: 2 (MODERATE)

INGREDIENTS

Cake
6 eggs, separated
¾ cup caster sugar
1½ cups plain flour
1½ tsp baking powder
2 tbsp rice bran oil
½ cup milk (optional)

Pour-over
1 can (395 g) condensed milk
1 cup evaporated milk
½ cup whole milk
1 tbsp vanilla extract
2 tbsp rum (optional)

Filling
300 ml fresh cream, whipped
1 cup cut fresh fruit (I like strawberries or mango)
¼ cup chopped almonds

Icing
150 g butter, softened
2 cups (600 g) icing sugar
2 tsp vanilla extract
4 tbsp milk (optional)
sprinkles (optional)

METHOD

Pre-heat oven to 175°C. Line a 30 cm round (or 25 cm square) cake tin with baking paper. Make sure it comes up the sides of the tin. Grease and flour the paper.

Beat egg whites until soft peaks can be formed when lifting the whisk, and set aside. In a separate bowl, beat egg yolks and sugar until pale and light and creamy. Add flour, baking powder and oil and fold in gently. If batter is too stiff, add up to ½ cup milk, until it reaches a soft runny batter consistency. Gently fold in egg white until incorporated.

Pour into prepared cake tin. Bake for 40–45 minutes or until a toothpick comes out clean when inserted.

While the cake cooks, blend condensed, evaporated and whole milks with vanilla and rum (if using). When the cake comes out of the oven, use a skewer or fork to poke the top of the cake to break the crust and allow easier absorption of the milks. Now slowly pour the milks onto it bit by bit, letting it absorb after each pour. Don't do it too fast, or the milks will just plunge to the bottom of the tin. It might look as if there is too much liquid, but the cake will absorb all of it. Refrigerate for at least 4 hours or, even better, overnight.

Turn cake out onto a cake plate and with a long knife cut it horizontally through the middle. Top bottom half with fresh whipped cream, fruit and almonds. Lay the top half carefully on top.

Make icing by beating all ingredients together until light and fluffy, adding milk to loosen it up if needed. Ice the top of the cake with a generous layer of icing – add sprinkles too if you like. Slice, eat and enjoy!

"Inspired by my love of condensed milk as well as my travels in Mexico, this 'tres leche' ('three milk') cake is the cake to beat all cakes. In Mexico it's a popular dessert for birthdays and weddings, but it's so irresistable I bake it whenever there's even the hint of celebration."

QUEEN ELIZABETH CAKE

Recipe by **NATALIE OLDFIELD**

MAKES: 1 CAKE | PREP TIME: 20 MINS | COOK TIME: 30–40 MINS | SKILL LEVEL: 1 (EASY)

INGREDIENTS

1 cup (125 g) dates, pitted and chopped
1 tsp baking soda
1 cup boiling water
1½ cups (210 g) plain flour
1 tsp baking powder
½ tsp salt
½ cup (40 g) chopped walnuts
65 g butter
1 cup (200 g) white sugar
1 egg
1 tsp vanilla essence

Topping

1 cup (80 g) toasted shredded coconut (see tip adjacent)
½ cup (90 g) firmly packed brown sugar
120 g butter
¼ cup cream

METHOD

Pre-heat oven to 180°C.

Mix dates with baking soda in a small bowl, pour boiling water over and set aside to cool.

Place flour, baking powder, salt and walnuts in a bowl and mix together.

Melt butter in a saucepan and cool, then add sugar, egg and vanilla, and whisk together. Add this mixture to the cooled dates and whisk to combine.

Fold the liquid mix into the dry mix until well combined, then pour into a greased and lined 23 cm cake tin.

Bake for 30–40 minutes or until cooked through – a skewer inserted into the centre should come out clean. Turn out onto a wire rack and leave to cool.

To make the topping, mix coconut, brown sugar, butter and cream in a saucepan on a medium heat. Bring to the boil and simmer for 4 minutes.

Allow mixture to cool down for approximately 10 minutes, then spread on cooled cake. Pre-heat oven grill to 180°C. Grill cake with topping for 3–5 minutes, or until golden. Cool and serve.

TIP

To toast coconut, spread on a baking tray and place in the oven at 180°C until golden, approximately 5 minutes.

"When I was a child I would run to my granny's cupboard to see if my favourite baking was there. When it was the Queen Elizabeth Cake I would be very disappointed! Nowadays I love this recipe so much I understand why my grandparents ate it with such delight."

RAISIN LOAF

Recipe by **TUI FLOWER**

SERVINGS: 8 | PREP TIME: 15 MINS | COOK TIME: 1 HOUR | SKILL LEVEL: 1 (EASY)

INGREDIENTS

1 cup milk
2 tbsp golden syrup
2 cups plain flour
3 tsp baking powder
pinch of salt
¾ cup sugar
1 cup raisins

METHOD

Pre-heat the oven to 180°C. Line the bottom of a 22 cm loaf tin with baking paper and grease the sides.

Put milk and golden syrup together in a pan and heat gently to combine. Leave to cool. Sift flour, baking powder and salt into a bowl, add sugar and raisins and stir to combine. Add the milk mixture, stirring to make a soft batter. Turn into the prepared tin.

Bake for about 1 hour. Allow to cool in the tin for 15–20 minutes, before removing to cool completely. Serve sliced, with or without buttering.

TIPS

This is a forgiving recipe; so, if you find measuring golden syrup tricky, a little inaccuracy will be allowed. It will also tolerate milk starting to sour.

"One of my earliest memories of learning to cook is helping my mother to make this raisin loaf. It has been a staple throughout my life."

CARROT CAKE WITH CREAM CHEESE FROSTING

Recipe by **RUTH PRETTY** *from Ruth Pretty Catering*

SERVINGS: 14–16 | PREP TIME: 20 MINS | COOK TIME: 1½ HOURS | SKILL LEVEL: 1 (EASY)

INGREDIENTS

420 g caster sugar
315 ml flavourless oil (e.g. canola)
2 tsp pure vanilla essence
2 tsp finely grated lemon zest
3 eggs, beaten lightly
270 g grated carrot
195 g peeled and grated apple
1 x 250 g tin unsweetened crushed pineapple, juice reserved
65 ml pineapple juice
40 g desiccated coconut
420 g plain flour
1 tsp ground cinnamon
2 tsp baking soda
½ tsp salt

Cream cheese frosting
375 g full-fat cream cheese
10 g butter, softened
2 tbsp lemon juice
1 tbsp, plus 1 tsp, finely grated lemon zest
375 g icing sugar

METHOD

Pre-heat the oven to 170°C. Lightly grease a 23 cm round cake tin with baking spray or additional oil. Line base with baking paper cut to fit.

Place sugar, oil, vanilla and lemon zest in a large bowl and use a hand whisk to mix together. (Do not use an electric mixer because it will create too much air.) Add eggs and mix well. Add carrot, apple, pineapple, juice and coconut and stir to combine.

Sift dry ingredients together, add to bowl and gently fold in.

Pour batter into prepared tin and bake for approximately 1½ hours or until a cake skewer inserted comes out clean, and the cake bounces back when you prod it. Remove from the oven. Place the tin on a wire rack and allow to cool for 10 minutes, then remove cake from the tin and place on a rack to cool completely.

In a medium-sized bowl, beat cream cheese until smooth and creamy. Dice butter and add with lemon juice and zest, and combine well.

Sift icing sugar into the bowl and beat until combined and the frosting is smooth. Use to ice cooled cake immediately or cover and refrigerate for up to one day, before icing.

TIPS

A peaky cream cheese frosting is too sweet for me – I prefer a citrusy flavour and I don't mind that it sits smooth and flat like this icing.

If you wish, garnish with culinary flowers such as thyme flowers, calendula petals, violas or nasturtiums.

RASPBERRY LAMINGTONS

Recipe by **KATE FAY** *from Cibo*

SERVINGS: 6 | PREP TIME: 30 MINS | COOK TIME: 35 MINS | SKILL LEVEL: 2 (MODERATE)

INGREDIENTS

Milk sponge

butter, for greasing

1 cup (200 g) plain flour, plus extra for dusting

1 tsp baking powder

pinch of salt

3 eggs, separated

⅔ cup (140 g) sugar

65 ml milk

½ tsp vanilla extract

Coconut crisps

50 g desiccated coconut

200 g caster sugar

20 g plain flour

100 g cream

Raspberry icing

125 g Valrhona Ivoire white chocolate

20 g butter

250 g icing sugar

½ cup milk

2 tbsp raspberry powder

To finish

1 cup desiccated coconut

whipped cream, for serving

a few fresh raspberries

METHOD

Pre-heat the oven to 180°C. Butter and flour a 16 cm x 26 cm sponge tin.

Sift flour, baking powder and salt into a bowl and set aside. Whisk egg whites with an electric mixer until frothy and then gradually add sugar, continuing to whisk until a stiff meringue forms. Reduce speed and add egg yolks, one at a time, whisking until just combined.

Fold milk and the flour mixture alternately into the egg mixture, then fold vanilla in. Pour into the prepared tin, then bake for 20–25 minutes or until the cake springs back when lightly pressed. Allow to cool, then cut into 12 small squares.

Leave the oven at 180°C for the coconut crisps. Line a baking tray with baking paper. Combine coconut, sugar and flour in a food processor. With the motor running, slowly pour in cream until it is incorporated.

Spread very thin strips of the coconut mixture on the baking paper (or spread all over the baking paper to create a single large biscuit), then bake for 8–10 minutes until golden and crisp. Cool on a wire rack. If you have baked a single sheet of biscuit, break it into smaller pieces.

For the icing, place chocolate and butter in a heatproof bowl set over a saucepan of simmering water. Heat, stirring, until melted and smooth. Remove bowl from the heat and stir in icing sugar, milk and raspberry powder, then whisk until smooth and combined.

To assemble, place desiccated coconut on a plate. Dip sponge squares in icing to coat, then roll in coconut. Serve lamingtons with whipped cream, whole raspberries and coconut crisps.

"This is an update on classic birthday party food from my childhood. The pink lamington was always my favourite and I remember peering through the bakery window to look at them."

KEV'S TOP LEMON DRIZZLE CAKE

Recipe by **KEVIN HOPGOOD** *from Hopgood's*

MAKES: 1 CAKE | PREP TIME: 20 MINS | COOK TIME: 40–50 MINS | SKILL LEVEL: 1 (EASY)

INGREDIENTS

225 g caster sugar
225 g butter, softened
few drops vanilla essence
4 eggs
225 g plain flour
1½ tsp baking powder
pinch of salt
zest of 1 lemon

Drizzle
juice of 2 lemons
90 g caster sugar

METHOD

Pre-heat oven to 180°C. Line a loaf tin (8 cm x 21 cm) with baking paper.

Beat caster sugar, butter and vanilla together until pale and creamy (about 5 minutes), then beat in eggs, one at a time. Sift in flour, baking powder and salt, add lemon zest and mix until well combined.

Spoon mix into prepared tin and level off. Bake for 40–50 minutes. Check that it is cooked by inserting a small knife or skewer into the centre of the cake – it should come out clean. Set aside in the tin once done.

Mix together lemon juice and caster sugar for the drizzle. Prick the cake (while it's still warm) with a skewer or fork, and pour the lemon syrup over the cake – it will soak in and also produce a lovely crisp topping.

Leave in the tin until cool, then remove and try to stop yourself from eating it (it's impossible).

TIPS

Don't share it.

You could use lime juice instead, or a combination of lemon and lime or orange and lemon. You could also add some Limoncello to the drizzle.

Would be great with homemade lemonade, or try Kev's Lemon Drop Martini: mix 45 ml vodka, 45 ml Limoncello, the juice of two lemons, 1 teaspoon of sugar and three mint leaves together with ice in a cocktail shaker. Divide between two glasses, top up with soda water, stir and add a slice of lemon.

"This recipe is a family favourite. Try to stop yourself from eating it – it's impossible!"

CHOCOLATE STOUT CAKE

Recipe by **SIMON HOLST**

SERVINGS: 10–12 | PREP TIME: 15 MINS | COOK TIME: 45–60 MINS | SKILL LEVEL: 1 (EASY)

INGREDIENTS

125 g butter
1 cup (175 g) dark chocolate melts
½ cup plain unsweetened yoghurt
2 large eggs
330 ml dark beer or stout
2 tsp vanilla essence
½ cup cocoa powder
1½ tsp baking soda
½ tsp salt
2 cups plain flour
1½ cups sugar

Icing

150 g good-quality dark chocolate, chopped
¼ cup sour cream

METHOD

Pre-heat oven to 180°C. Spray a 22 cm springform cake tin with non-stick spray and line with baking paper.

Measure butter and chocolate into a small pot and heat gently until melted. Whisk yoghurt and eggs together in a large bowl, then add stout, vanilla and the chocolate/butter mixture. Stir to combine.

Sift cocoa, baking soda, salt and flour over the liquids and sprinkle sugar on top. Stir until evenly mixed. Pour into prepared tin and bake for 45–60 minutes or until a skewer inserted into the middle comes out clean. Turn out onto a rack to cool.

For the icing: gently heat dark chocolate with sour cream until just melted, then stir until smooth and glossy.

Cover cake with icing. Leave to stand until the icing is firm (it will never set completely), then serve as is or with yoghurt or lightly whipped cream.

"This moist, dark cake is perfect for a dinner party dessert or other special occasion."

ALMOND CAKE

Recipe by **LOIS DAISH**

MAKES: 1 CAKE | PREP TIME: 15 MINS | COOK TIME: 35 MINS | SKILL LEVEL: 1 (EASY)

INGREDIENTS

200 g butter, softened
200 g caster sugar
4 eggs, at room temperature
½ tsp almond essence
½ tsp vanilla essence
150 g plain flour
¾ tsp baking powder
100 g ground almonds (or almond meal)
¼ cup milk

METHOD

Before you begin, ensure that the butter is soft and the eggs are at room temperature. Pre-heat the oven to 175°C. Take a square or round baking tin, about 20 cm across, butter it lightly and line the bottom with baking paper.

Cream the butter and sugar together until very pale and light. Beat in the eggs, one at a time. Add the almond and vanilla essences.

Sift the flour and baking powder and mix with the ground almonds. Gently fold into the butter and sugar mixture, alternating with the milk. When all is thoroughly mixed, scoop into the baking tin. Bake for 35–45 minutes, until a fork comes away clean when inserted into the middle of the cake. The cake will smell delicious and be golden-brown on top.

Serve as soon as cooled, or keep in a covered container for several days.

"Towards the end of her life, this was the only cake my mother, Dorothy, ever made. With its rich flavour and moist, nutty texture, this delicious cake needs no adornment."

ORANGE CAKE WITH PŌHUTUKAWA HONEY-ROASTED STONE FRUITS

Recipe by **SHAUN CLOUSTON** *from Logan Brown*

SERVINGS: 6 | PREP TIME: 30 MINS | COOK TIME: 3 HOURS | SKILL LEVEL: 2 (MODERATE)

INGREDIENTS

Orange cake

2 oranges
6 eggs
225 g sugar
225 g ground almonds
1 tsp baking powder
unsweetened organic Greek yoghurt, to serve

Roasted stone fruits

200 g sugar
400 ml water
50 g pōhutukawa honey
2 tbsp brandy
6 golden peaches, white nectarines or apricots

GF

METHOD

Orange cake: boil whole oranges for 2 hours. Remove from the pan, cool a little, then purée and sieve. Grease and line a 20 cm round cake tin.

Pre-heat the oven to 150°C. Lightly whisk eggs and sugar together, then whisk in puréed oranges, ground almonds and baking powder. Pour mix into the cake tin. Bake for about 35–40 minutes, or until a skewer inserted into the cake comes out clean.

Let the cake sit for about 10 minutes before turning out of the tin.

Roasted stone fruits: these can be prepared while the oranges are boiling. Pre-heat the oven to 190°C. Gently heat together sugar, water, honey and brandy in a saucepan over a low heat, until sugar and honey are dissolved. Bring to the boil, and then remove from the heat.

Halve the stone fruit and remove the stones. Place fruit, flat side up, in an ovenproof dish and evenly cover with the pōhutukawa honey syrup. Place in the oven to bake, basting the fruit with the syrup every 5 minutes or so. Bake until fruit is soft but still holding its shape and just beginning to colour. The time will vary depending on the ripeness of the fruit, but should be approximately 12–15 minutes.

Serve slices of warm cake with warm roasted stone fruit and a little syrup drizzled over, plus a good dollop of yoghurt.

TIP

You can roast the stone fruits ahead of time as they keep well in the fridge – warm gently in a small saucepan before serving.

DATE LOAF

Recipe by **CARA BAYLY**

SERVES: 8–10 | PREP TIME: 10 MINS, PLUS STANDING | COOK TIME: 40–45 MINS | SKILL LEVEL: 1 (EASY)

INGREDIENTS

- 1 cup tightly packed dates
- 1 tsp baking soda
- 1 big tbsp butter
- 1 cup boiling water
- ½ cup (90 g) coconut sugar (or brown sugar)
- 1 egg
- 2 cups (310 g) plain flour
- 1 tsp baking powder
- ½ cup chocolate chips (optional)
- ¼ cup mixed seeds for topping (optional)

METHOD

Put dates, baking soda and butter in a bowl and cover with boiling water. Set aside until cool (about 1 hour).

Pre-heat oven to 180°C. Line a 22 cm loaf pan with non-stick baking paper.

Place cooled date mixture in a blender or food processer and blitz until super-smooth. Return to the bowl and beat in sugar and egg. Sift in flour and baking powder, and add chocolate chips if using. Stir to combine.

Pour into loaf pan and bake at for about 45 minutes, until a skewer poked into the middle comes out clean. Cool in the tin for ten minutes, then turn out.

VARIATIONS

For a sweet variation, add chocolate chips in with the flour and baking powder.

To make a savoury version sprinkle the top of the loaf before baking with mixed raw seeds – I often use pumpkin, sunflower and sesame seeds.

"This is my take on the traditional date loaf. My kids have an aversion to 'bits' in their food so I purée the dates to remove the offending chunks."

DELUXE CHOCOLATE CAKE

Recipe by **DEAN BRETTSCHNEIDER**

SERVINGS: 8 | PREP TIME: 25 MINS | COOK TIME: 45 MINS, PLUS STANDING | SKILL LEVEL: 2 (MODERATE)

INGREDIENTS

Chocolate cake

160 g milk
¾ tsp cream of tartar
80 g oil
2 small eggs
1 tsp vanilla extract
180 g plain flour
70 g cocoa powder
290 g caster sugar
1 tsp baking soda
½ tsp baking powder
100 g hot water

Ganache filling and coating

150 ml fresh cream
300 g chocolate, chopped finely

Decoration

1 large packet Maltesers
icing sugar, for dusting

METHOD

Pre-heat the oven to 180°C. Butter and flour a 20 cm round, high-sided cake tin.

Place milk and cream of tartar in a small glass; stir and set aside for 5 minutes. In a bowl, place oil, eggs and vanilla, and stir to combine.

Sift flour, cocoa, sugar, baking soda and baking powder into a large bowl. Add the milk/cream of tartar solution to the oil, egg and vanilla mixture and stir, then add to the dry ingredients. Using a hand-beater, mix to combine, then slowly add hot water and mix well, until you have a smooth batter.

Pour the mixture into the prepared tin and bake for approximately 45 minutes, until a cake skewer comes out clean when inserted. Cool for 15 minutes in the tin, then remove and cool completely on a wire rack. Once cool, enclose in plastic wrap and keep overnight for best results and finish it the following day.

To make the ganache, place cream in a saucepan and gently bring to the boil. Remove from the heat and add chocolate. Stir, using a wooden spoon, until chocolate has melted. Cool a little, then beat with the wooden spoon until ganache filling has begun to thicken slightly.

Unwrap the cake from the day before and rub the palm of your hand on the cake's edges to remove any loose crumbs. Place the cake on the work surface, then use a palette knife held vertically to coat the outer sides of the cake with the ganache, ensuring that there is an even coating all round.

Now, holding the palette knife horizontally, spread a layer of ganache on the top surface of the cake, making sure that you have an even coating. Use the palette knife to lift the cake up and gently place it on a large, flat serving plate.

While the ganache is still fresh, arrange the Maltesers around the top surface of the cake and lightly dust the top with icing sugar.

"This chocolate cake is super simple to bake so it's my go-to fail-safe cake, no matter where I am in the world."

CHOCOLATE LAMINGTON MUD CAKES

Recipe by **KATE FAY** *from Cibo*

MAKES: 8 | PREP TIME: 35 MINS | COOK TIME: 12–15 MINS | SKILL LEVEL: 2 (MODERATE)

INGREDIENTS

Lamingtons

225 g unsalted butter

320 g good-quality dark chocolate

6 eggs, separated

135 g caster sugar

100 g plain flour, sifted

100 g long-thread dessiccated coconut

Chocolate ganache icing

1 cup cream

200 g good-quality dark chocolate

METHOD

Pre-heat oven to 150°C. Butter and flour eight small brioche moulds or a muffin tin.

Melt butter and chocolate in a metal bowl set over a saucepan of simmering water.

In a separate bowl, beat egg yolks and sugar until thick and pale, about 5–8 minutes. Fold into the butter and chocolate mixture, then add flour – it should be quite a thick consistency. In another bowl, whisk the egg whites until they form soft peaks when you lift the whisk, then fold into the chocolate mixture.

Pour batter into the moulds to fill three-quarters of the way up the sides, and bake for 12–15 minutes. Take care not to over-cook, as the insides of the cakes should be slightly soft. Cool cakes in their moulds and turn out when cool.

For the ganache icing, bring cream to the boil in a small saucepan. Melt chocolate in a bowl set over a saucepan of simmering water. When chocolate has melted, whisk the hot cream through. Set aside, keeping warm.

Toast coconut in a dry frying pan over a medium heat until mostly golden-brown. Set aside to cool.

Place cakes on a wire rack and coat with icing. Sprinkle cakes with toasted coconut.

TIP

These cakes are delicious served with whipped cream or coconut ice cream.

CRUNCHY-TOPPED FEIJOA & WALNUT CAKE

Recipe by **NATALIE OLDFIELD**

SERVINGS: 8 | PREP TIME: 15 MINS | COOK TIME: 1¼ HOURS | SKILL LEVEL: 1 (EASY)

INGREDIENTS

Cake

2 cups self-raising flour
½ cup wholemeal flour
1 tsp ground cinnamon
½ tsp ground nutmeg
1 cup sugar
185 g butter, melted
½ cup water
3 eggs, beaten lightly
1½ cups chopped fresh feijoa flesh
½ cup chopped walnuts

Topping

60 g butter
½ cup brown sugar
¼ tsp ground cinnamon
¼ tsp ground nutmeg
½ cup chopped walnuts

METHOD

Pre-heat the oven to 180°C. Grease and line a 20 cm round or square cake tin.

Sift the flours and spices into a large bowl and stir in the sugar. In a separate bowl, mix together butter, water and eggs. Add wet ingredients to flour mix and fold together. Lastly, fold in feijoa and walnuts. Pour into tin.

For the topping, melt butter and mix in the other ingredients. Pour over cake mixture and cook for 1¼ hours. Cool in the tin.

"My mum's specialty is this delicious, wholesome recipe. Feijoa season only comes once a year, but when it does we can't wait to eat this cake warm with plenty of cream."

RICH CHRISTMAS CAKE

Recipe by **LAURAINE JACOBS**

MAKES: 60 | PREP TIME: 30 MINS, PLUS STANDING | COOK TIME: 4 HOURS | SKILL LEVEL: 2 (MODERATE)

INGREDIENTS

1½ kg mixed dried fruit, including sultanas, raisins and currants
500 g butter
385 g brown sugar
8 eggs
1 tbsp golden syrup
4 tbsp blackcurrant jam
500 g flour
1 tsp baking soda
1 tsp baking powder
½ tsp salt
1 tsp mixed spice
1 tsp ground cinnamon
150 g glacé cherries
100 g almonds, blanched
¼ cup dark rum or brandy
apricot jam (optional)

METHOD

Place all the dried fruit in a large saucepan and cover with water. Bring to a boil and simmer for 5 minutes. Drain well, cool and let stand overnight.

Pre-heat the oven to 160°C.

Beat butter and sugar well until light and creamy, then add eggs one at a time, beating well between each addition so they are well incorporated. Add golden syrup and blackcurrant jam and beat that in well too.

Sift dry ingredients together four times. Add the dry ingredients and fruit in small alternate batches to the creamed butter, sugar and egg mixture, and finally fold in the cherries.

Line a 24 cm cake tin with several layers of greaseproof paper and tip in the mixture. Press almonds onto the surface.

Bake the cake for 4 hours. When cooked, pour dark rum or brandy over the surface while the cake is still warm. Cool, and place in an airtight container to mature for 2–4 weeks.

Immediately before cutting the cake, glaze the top with melted apricot jam for a professional-looking finish.

"This Christmas cake has been one of our family traditions for as long as I can remember. I don't know where Nana Laura got the recipe from, but it must be over one hundred years old as my my ninety-year-old mother has been baking it all her life."

BANANA CAKE

Recipe by **JO SEAGAR**

SERVINGS: 10 | PREP TIME: 15 MINS | COOK TIME: 50–60 MINS | SKILL LEVEL: 1 (EASY)

INGREDIENTS

1½ cups sugar
150 g butter, softened
4 eggs
3 bananas, mashed
¾ cup milk
1 tsp baking soda
200 ml plain natural yoghurt
2½ cups plain flour
3 tsp baking powder

Lemon icing

25 g butter
juice and grated zest of 1 lemon
2–2½ cups icing sugar

METHOD

Pre-heat the oven to 160°C. Spray a 23 cm round springform tin with baking spray. Line the base with baking paper.

Beat sugar and butter together until creamy and pale. Add eggs and beat until thick and creamy and well incorporated. Add bananas and mix in well.

Heat milk in a small saucepan or microwave-proof bowl until nearly boiling. Stir baking soda into milk and then stir this into the banana mixture. Add yoghurt, flour and baking powder. Mix well and pour into the prepared cake tin.

Bake for 50–60 minutes until the cake is cooked in the middle and just pulling away from the sides of the tin. Cool in the tin for 5 minutes, then release the spring sides and cool completely on a wire rack.

For the icing, place butter, lemon juice and zest in a small microwave-proof jug or bowl. Microwave on high for 30–40 seconds until the butter is melted.

Beat in enough icing sugar to make a smooth icing. Spread over the completely cooled cake and allow to drip down the sides.

BLACK DORIS PLUM & ALMOND TORTE

Recipe by **CAZNA GILDER** *from Mrs Clark's Cafe*

SERVINGS: 6 | PREP TIME: 10 MINS | COOK TIME: 40 MINS | SKILL LEVEL: 1 (EASY)

INGREDIENTS

3 Black Doris plums
8 egg whites
2 cups ground almonds
¾ cup icing sugar, sifted
50 g butter, melted
100 g slivered almonds

GF

METHOD

Pre-heat the oven to 170°C. Grease and line a 20 cm round cake tin.

Cut plums in half and remove the stones. Whisk egg whites until soft peaks form. Add almonds, icing sugar and butter and fold until combined. Add half the batter to the tin, and place your halved plums on top. Then top with the rest of the batter. *BANG!* Done... It's best not to let the wet mix sit around, so work quickly and bake straight away.

Bake for 40 minutes, until torte springs back when touched. Serve warm with natural yoghurt, and toasted flaked almonds and icing sugar for prettiness. *ENJOY!*

TIPS

Just about any fruit can be used: fresh or tinned, cherries, tamarillos, gooseberries. Best served with a dollop of natural yoghurt – and it's healthy, even!

"This torte has the look of an old-school tea cake and can be whipped up very quickly – and it's gluten free!"

CHOCOLATE SPONGE

Recipe by **DEAN BRETTSCHNEIDER**

SERVINGS: 6–8 | PREP TIME: 30 MINS | COOK TIME: 25–30 MINS | SKILL LEVEL: 2 (MODERATE)

INGREDIENTS

400 g cream

100 g good-quality dark chocolate, chopped into small pieces

5 eggs, at room temperature

150 g caster sugar

150 g plain flour

5 g (1 tsp) baking powder

50 g cocoa powder

50 g butter, melted

To decorate

50 g good-quality dark chocolate, grated into shavings

1 punnet each: fresh strawberries, raspberries, blueberries

icing sugar

METHOD

The day before, place cream in a saucepan and heat to blood temperature. Add chopped chocolate and stir until chocolate has completely melted. Put in a container, cover and place in the refrigerator to chill. The next day, whip until soft/medium peaks form and use when required.

Pre-heat the oven to 190°C. Grease and flour a 20 cm round cake tin.

In an electric mixer and using the whisk attachment, whisk together eggs and sugar to the ribbon stage (this is when the mixture is thick, and when trailed on itself it will hold its own weight for about 10 seconds before sinking into the mixture).

Sift flour, baking powder and cocoa together, then carefully fold through egg/sugar foam mixture. Once flour is three-quarters folded through, add butter and continue to fold through gently. Avoid over-mixing at this stage or you will lose all the precious air bubbles you have created.

Immediately place the mixture in the prepared cake tin. Bake until sponge is set, approximately 25–30 minutes. Cool completely in the tin.

When cool, remove cake from tin and cut horizontally into three equal-sized layers. Spread a layer of chocolate whipped cream on one layer of sponge, then place the next layer of sponge on top and press down lightly.

Spread a second layer of chocolate whipped cream on top of the second sponge layer, then top with the final layer of the sponge and press down lightly again.

Finally, spread remaining chocolate whipped cream on top and sprinkle with dark chocolate shavings. Arrange fresh berries on top. Lightly sprinkle with icing sugar.

"Chocolate cream, chocolate sponge, chocolate shavings and fresh summer berries – you simply can't go wrong, can you?"

FRENCH VANILLA & BERRY MINI CAKES

Recipe by **JULIE LE CLERC**

MAKES: 12 | PREP TIME: 10 MINS | COOK TIME: 20–25 MINS | SKILL LEVEL: 1 (EASY)

INGREDIENTS

1½ cups icing sugar
½ cup plain flour
1 cup desiccated coconut
175 g butter
6 egg whites
pinch of salt
1 tsp vanilla extract
1½ cups berries (fresh or frozen)
extra icing sugar, to dust

METHOD

Pre-heat the oven to 190°C. Grease 12 individual patty pan or muffin tins, of ½ cup capacity.

Sift icing sugar and flour into a mixing bowl and add coconut. Melt butter and lightly beat egg whites with salt. Add butter, egg whites and vanilla to the mixing bowl and stir well to combine – expect the mixture to be quite runny.

Spoon mixture into prepared tins to fill by two-thirds. Top each mini cake with a few berries, pressing these into the surface.

Bake for 25 minutes or until well browned on the outside and cooked in the middle when tested – a skewer inserted into the centre of one mini cake should come out clean.

Remove to stand in tins for 5 minutes before turning out onto a cooling rack. Dust with icing sugar and serve with whipped cream or yoghurt on the side, if desired.

These mini cakes are lovely enjoyed with a nice cup of tea or coffee, but can also double as dessert.

TIPS

The berries can be raspberries, blueberries, blackberries, or a mixture.

If you prefer, substitute the same quantity of ground almonds for the coconut.

DAME ALISON HOLST

MUFFINS, SCONES & PASTRIES

PIKELETS

Recipe by **DAME ALISON HOLST**

SERVINGS: 4 | PREP TIME: 4 MINS | COOK TIME: 15–20 MINS | SKILL LEVEL: 1 (EASY)

INGREDIENTS

1 rounded tbsp golden syrup
25 g butter
1 tbsp sugar
½ cup milk
1 large egg
1 cup self-raising flour

METHOD

Heat a frying pan. (Use a high heat setting if the frying pan is electric.) Dip an ordinary tablespoon in hot water and use to measure the golden syrup into a bowl. Add butter and warm to soften both (microwaving is easiest), then mix in sugar, milk and egg. Sprinkle or sieve flour over the top, then mix in briefly with a whisk or beater just until smooth.

Rub the surface of the hot frying pan with a little butter on a paper towel. Drop dessertspoon or tablespoon lots of mixture into the pan, pouring mixture off the tip of the spoon. If the mixture is too thick and doesn't spread easily, add a little extra milk to it.

Turn pikelets over as soon as bubbles begin to burst on the surface. (Turn heat up if the cooked sides are not brown enough OR turn heat down if they brown too much by the time the first bubbles burst.) Cook the second side until the centres spring back when touched with your finger.

Cook in batches until all the batter is used. Keep cooked pikelets warm between the folds of a clean tea towel. Serve soon after making – spread with butter and jam, top butter with hundreds and thousands for small children, or 'dress them up' with whipped cream, jam and fresh berries. Yum!

"Pikelets are a simple, inexpensive food. They don't take very long to make, and everyone likes them."

CHELSEA BUNS

Recipe by **MICHAEL COUGHLIN** *from Olivers at the Victoria Store*

MAKES: 12 | PREP TIME: 30 MINS, PLUS RISING | COOK TIME: 15–20 MINS | SKILL LEVEL: 2 (MODERATE)

INGREDIENTS

Dough

500 g high-grade flour
30 g caster sugar
7 g sachet dried yeast
1 tsp salt
300 ml milk
40 g unsalted butter, softened
water, for brushing

Filling

⅔ cup (100 g) currants
¾ cup (100 g) sultanas
75 g soft brown sugar
2 tsp ground cinnamon
30 g butter, melted

To finish

1 egg, beaten
2 tbsp milk
2 tbsp caster sugar

METHOD

For the dough: sift flour, caster sugar, yeast and salt into a large bowl. Warm milk in a saucepan to lukewarm (around 36°C).

Make a well in the middle of flour mixture. Add milk and stir until the contents of the bowl come together as a soft dough.

Tip dough onto a generously floured work surface. Knead for 10 minutes, adding more flour if necessary, until dough is smooth and elastic and no longer feels sticky. Alternatively, use a cake mixer with a dough hook and develop/knead the dough on a medium speed for 6–8 minutes, or until dough is soft and silky.

Place dough in a large bowl and cover with plastic wrap, or use a lightly oiled plastic container with a tight-fitting lid. Set aside in a warm place for 1 hour, or until dough has doubled in size. Knock dough back to its original size and turn out onto a lightly floured work surface. Roll dough out into a rectangle, about ½ cm thick and with the length at least four times the width (e.g. 80 cm x 20 cm). Have the long edge at the front of the work surface.

For the filling: mix the fruit, sugar and cinnamon together. Brush dough with a little water and sprinkle fruit filling over, leaving a clear 2 cm edge furthest away from you to allow it to stick properly when rolled up. Roll up tightly from the front long edge, as you would a Swiss roll, making sure the final edge of the dough has enough water to seal and stick the dough together so it doesn't come apart during cutting or baking. Grease and flour a large baking sheet.

Brush the roll with melted butter, then use a sharp knife to cut the roll straight through into 12 even pieces. Place dough pieces cut-side down onto the baking sheet, allowing about 2 cm of space between them. Cover buns with lightly oiled plastic wrap, so as not to let the dough surface dry out at all. Place in a warm area of the kitchen until buns are nearly doubled in size (at a room temperature of around 21°C this should take about 40 minutes).

To finish: pre-heat oven to 190°C. When buns have almost doubled in size, brush carefully with beaten egg and bake for 15–20 minutes until buns are an even golden-brown colour.

To make a glaze, heat milk and sugar in a saucepan until boiling. Reduce the heat and simmer for 2–3 minutes. Remove buns from oven and brush with glaze, then set aside to cool on a wire rack.

SPICED APPLE, WALNUT & DATE MUFFINS

Recipe by **CAZNA GILDER** *from Mrs Clark's Cafe*

MAKES: 6 LARGE OR 12 STANDARD MUFFINS | PREP TIME: 15 MINS | COOK TIME: 15–25 MINS | SKILL LEVEL: 1 (EASY)

INGREDIENTS

1 cup (150 g) chopped dates
1 cup apple juice
2½ cups plain flour
3 tsp baking powder
½ tsp ground cinnamon
½ tsp mixed spice
¼ tsp salt (or a pinch)
½ cup brown sugar
2 medium-sized (Eve) apples, grated (I like the skin left on!)
50 g butter, melted
1 large egg
½ cup milk
½ cup unsweetened natural yoghurt

Crunchy topping

25 g butter, softened
¼ cup brown sugar
½ tsp mixed spice
½ cup finely chopped walnuts

METHOD

Pre-heat oven to 190°C. Grease the holes of a large or standard muffin tin, or line with paper cases.

Place dates and apple juice in a saucepan and bring to the boil. Cool slightly, then drain, keeping the liquid.

Sift flour, baking powder, spices and salt together into a large bowl. Add sugar and stir to mix.

Mix grated apple, butter, egg, milk, yoghurt and ¼ cup of date/apple liquid together well. Add to dry ingredients and fold together gently until just combined. Spoon into muffin tin.

Mix topping ingredients together well. Sprinkle topping over muffins and bake for 15 minutes (standard muffins) or 25 minutes (large muffins). Cool on a wire rack.

DOUGHNUTS WITH CRÈME DIPLOMAT

Recipe by **KIM EVANS** *from Little & Friday*

MAKES: ABOUT 15 | PREP TIME: 1½–2 HOURS | COOK TIME: 30 MINS | SKILL LEVEL: 2 (MODERATE)

INGREDIENTS

Brioche dough

550 ml milk

60 g fresh yeast (crumbled) or 3 tsp dry yeast

½ cup sugar

6½ cups plain flour

3 tsp salt

3 eggs

140 g unsalted butter

Crème diplomat (makes 2½ cups)

250 ml milk

½ tsp vanilla essence or paste

¼ cup caster sugar

2 egg yolks

2 tbsp cornflour

150 ml cream

To finish

oil, for frying

raspberry coulis or jam

a large bowlful of icing sugar, for dusting

METHOD

For the dough: heat milk over a medium heat until lukewarm. Remove from heat and pour over yeast, stirring until yeast has dissolved.

Place dry ingredients in a mixing bowl. Using an electric mixer with a dough hook, mix at low speed (or mix by hand) to combine fully. Add milk/yeast mixture and eggs to the bowl, continuing to mix at low speed until a sticky dough forms. Stop the mixer.

Scrape down the dough and then turn the mixer speed on to medium for 10 minutes until an elastic, shiny dough forms and pulls away from the bowl. If doing this by hand, knead the dough on a lightly floured surface.

Cut butter into small pieces and gradually knead into the mixture until well combined. Cover the bowl with a tea towel and allow dough to rise until almost doubled in size. Tip dough onto a floured surface – it is now ready to use.

For the crème diplomat: while the dough is rising make the crème diplomat. Combine milk, vanilla and half the caster sugar in a saucepan, and bring to the boil. In a separate bowl, beat together remaining caster sugar and egg yolks until pale and thick. Slowly pour half the milk mixture into the egg mixture, whisking constantly.

Return remaining milk mixture to the heat. When it has reached boiling point, leave on the heat and quickly add the egg mixture, whisking constantly. Keep whisking vigorously until it returns to the boil, then remove from the heat. Pour into a bowl and place a circle of baking paper on top, to stop a film forming on the surface. Cool, then chill. (This is called crème pâtissière.)

Whip cream until firm. Beat chilled crème pâtissière until smooth and fold gently through cream with a metal spoon. Can be refrigerated in an airtight container for up to three days.

For the doughnuts: roll dough out on a floured surface to 4 cm thick. Using a cookie cutter, cut into circles. Allow to prove for 10–15 minutes – it is ready when a dry skin forms on the dough.

In a large saucepan, add oil to 2 cm deep and heat to 180°C. It is best to use a thermometer to get the temperature just right. If you are not using one, heat the oil over a medium heat – once it starts smoking, it is too hot. Drop a few doughnuts into the hot oil at a time. You do not want them to touch, or they will stick together. Cook for 3 minutes on each side, until they are quite dark and crisp. Remove and allow to cool on a wire rack covered with baking paper.

Once cool, poke a hole into each doughnut, creating a cavity. Fill a piping bag with raspberry coulis or jam and squeeze about 1 teaspoon's worth into each cavity. Next, use a clean piping bag full of crème diplomat to fill each doughnut until it starts to expand. Dust each doughnut generously with icing sugar.

"I'm big on sharing recipes; the more people who are inspired to cook, the better! I hope you enjoy making the dough from scratch."

BUTTERMILK PANCAKES WITH VANILLA-BAKED BLUEBERRIES & RICOTTA

Recipe by **TOM HUTCHISON** *from WBC/Capitol*

SERVINGS: 4–6 | PREP TIME: 5 MINS | COOK TIME: 30–40 MINS | SKILL LEVEL: I (EASY)

INGREDIENTS

Vanilla-baked blueberries
500 g frozen blueberries
250 g white sugar
1 tsp vanilla paste

Pancakes
250 g plain flour
20 g baking powder
5 g baking soda
pinch of salt
40 g butter
4 large (size 7) free-range eggs
600 ml buttermilk
250 ml clarified butter, for cooking
400 g tub of good-quality ricotta
100 g icing sugar, for dusting
200 ml maple syrup, to drizzle

METHOD

For the vanilla-baked blueberries: pre-heat the oven to 180°C. Shake frozen berries in sugar and vanilla paste to coat, then cook them, uncovered, in the oven for 30–40 minutes, until their skins have started to blister and any moisture has evaporated. Cool to room temperature.

For the pancakes: sift flour, baking powder, baking soda and salt into a large bowl. Melt butter and place in a separate bowl. Whisk eggs, buttermilk and melted butter together.

Fold wet ingredients into the dry ones. Adjust the texture to a thick pouring consistency by adding more flour or buttermilk as required.

Pre-heat the oven to 220°C.

Heat a 20 cm heavy-bottomed, ovenproof frying pan over a moderate to high heat. Once the pan is hot, add 3 tablespoons of clarified butter.

Once the pan is sizzling, place 1 large ladleful (¾ cup) of pancake mix into the centre of the pan and allow it to spread naturally. Fry the pancake for about 30 seconds, then transfer it to the middle of the hot oven. Once bubbles have formed on the surface, indicating that the pancake is cooking through (about 3–4 minutes), remove the pancake and flip it over. Return the pan to the oven and allow the other side to cook, until both sides are golden-brown and the cake bounces back in the centre when pressed.

To serve, stack your pancakes on a warm plate. Top it with a dessertspoon of fresh ricotta and a generous serve of vanilla-baked blueberries. Dust with icing sugar and drizzle with maple syrup. Enjoy.

"I like to cook pancakes for the family on a Saturday morning. We spend some quality time together as we chow down and chat about anything and everything."

CROISSANTS

Recipe by **JIM BYARS** *from The Friday Shop*

MAKES: ABOUT 20 | PREP TIME: 2 HOURS, PLUS PROVING
COOK TIME: 15–20 MINS | SKILL LEVEL: 3 (MORE CHALLENGING)

INGREDIENTS

1 kg high-grade flour
500 ml milk, lukewarm
100 g sugar
100 g egg
13 g instant dried yeast
500 g butter, chilled

METHOD

Make a dough using flour, milk, sugar, egg and yeast. Mix until smooth – usually I leave the dough covered in the refrigerator overnight to prove.

Lightly pat butter out to a flat rectangle. Take dough and knead it a little, then roll into a rectangle. Place butter on one half of this and fold the other half of the dough over the butter to enclose it completely. Press the edges closed and gently roll the dough into a rectangle again.

Fold one-third of the dough over, then fold one-third at the opposite end over the top (single turn); roll lightly to press the layers together and rest in the refrigerator for at least 15 minutes. With the long side facing you, roll the dough out to a rectangle again. Fold one side of the dough into the centre, then fold the other side in to meet it, then fold dough in half, like closing a book (double turn). Roll lightly to press layers together and rest again in the refrigerator for at least 15 minutes.

Give the dough another single turn, and allow to rest in the refrigerator for 30 minutes. Pre-heat the oven to 180°C.

Roll the dough out to a rectangle 2½ mm thick, at least 20 cm wide. Using a large knife, cut triangles 10 cm across the base and 20 cm high. Roll up to form your croissants and place on a baking tray. Prove until doubled in size (about 2 hours) and bake for 15–20 minutes, until golden. (Note that this recipe can easily be halved.)

APPLE STRUDEL

Recipe by the team at **THE CLAREVILLE BAKERY**

SERVES: 6 | PREP TIME: 1 ½ HOURS, PLUS CHILLING | COOK TIME: 20–25 MINS | SKILL LEVEL: 2 (MODERATE)

INGREDIENTS

Puff pastry
- 500 g plain flour
- 2 tsp salt
- 40 g butter
- 220 ml chilled water
- 330 g butter for rolling
- 1 egg, beaten

Apple filling
- approx. 4 apples, preferably green (400 g when prepared)
- 30 g sugar
- 50 g currants
- a few drops of vanilla extract
- pinch of ground cassia or cinnamon
- 1 tbsp Cointreau or orange juice
- 30 g butter
- 30 ml water
- 1 tsp cornflour

Apricot glaze
- 100 g apricot jam
- 1 tbsp water

METHOD

Dough: place flour, salt, 40 g butter and chilled water in a mixing bowl and use your hands to combine together to form a rough mass. Tip onto a clean work surface and continue mixing till fully combined and smooth, about 10 minutes. Do not over-mix or knead. The dough will be quite firm, but don't be tempted to add more liquid to it as it will then be too soft later on. Once dough is fully mixed, press it out into a square, wrap in plastic wrap and chill in the refrigerator for 30 minutes (or up to 24 hours).

Place extra butter between two sheets of plastic wrap and use a rolling pin to knock the butter into a square 1 cm thick (approximately 15 cm x 15 cm). Chill – it needs to be firm but malleable. Place chilled dough on a lightly floured work surface and roll into a square 1 cm thick (approximately 25 cm x 25 cm). Place butter onto dough with the corners of the butter just inside the straight sides of the dough. Fold the corners of the dough into the centre of the butter, encasing the butter fully. You should now have two layers of dough and one layer of butter inside the dough layers. Roll pastry into a rectangle, approximately 1–1.5 cm thick. The length should be approximately three times the width. Now imagine the pastry divided into three parts. Fold one end of the pastry two-thirds of the way towards the other end, then fold the other end over the first fold to give three even layers. This is called a 'single turn'. Cover dough with plastic wrap and chill for 30 minutes. Repeat the rolling and folding and chill for another 30 minutes. Repeat two more times; you should now have given the pastry four single turns. Chill pastry for a further 30 minutes before the final rolling.

Filling: Core and peel apples and slice thinly. Place in a saucepan with sugar, currants, vanilla, spice and Cointreau or orange juice, and bring to the boil. Turn down to a simmer and cook, stirring, until apples are beginning to soften. Add butter and stir through until combined. Mix cornflour and water together, add to apple mixture and simmer gently, stirring until thickened; apples should be soft but not over-cooked. Remove from the heat and allow to cool.

Remove pastry from refrigerator, divide in half and roll out each half to a final thickness of 3 mm (30 cm x 22 cm for each piece). Use as little flour as possible to roll it out. Cut into six 10 cm squares (for the bottoms of the strudels) plus six 12 cm x 10 cm pieces (for the tops). In the tops, make five or six cuts through the pastry, starting 2 cm in from the longer side and going across to 2 cm in from the other edge, making a sort of ladder pattern.

Scoop a couple of spoonsful of apple filling onto the bottom pieces of pastry, making a fat sausage shape from one end to the other. Leave 2 cm of pastry clear on each side. Brush pastry with water and then cover with the top pieces of pastry, with the cuts running along the sausage of fruit filling. The uncut edges of the top should marry with the wetted bottom pastry. Press gently to stick together. Brush tops with beaten egg and allow to rest in the refrigerator for 30 minutes. Pre-heat oven to 200°C. Brush tops again with egg and bake for 20–25 minutes or until golden brown. Don't be afraid to get plenty of colour on the pastry. Cool strudels on a wire rack.

Make glaze by heating apricot jam with water in a small saucepan until combined. Strain. Brush cooled strudels with some apricot glaze. Serve warmed.

BLUEBERRY, ORANGE & WHITE CHOCOLATE MUFFINS

Recipe by the team at **BOSCO CAFÉ**

MAKES: 18 | PREP TIME: 10 MINS | COOK TIME: 30–35 MINS | SKILL LEVEL: 1 (EASY)

INGREDIENTS

4 oranges
1¼ cups sugar
1¼ cups soya oil
1 tsp vanilla essence
4 eggs
1¼ cups yoghurt
1¾ cups milk
8 cups self-raising flour
2 tsp baking soda
pinch of salt
3 cups frozen berries – blueberries, blackberries or raspberries
3 cups white chocolate buttons
extra chocolate and berries, for topping

METHOD

Pre-heat the oven to 150°C. Peel oranges and remove pips from the segments. Place everything, including the peel, into blender and blend until mushy. Add sugar, oil, vanilla, eggs, yoghurt and milk and blend together.

In a large bowl, sift flour, baking soda and salt together. Mix in wet ingredients and add berries and chocolate.

Spoon into lightly greased muffin tins using a wide-mouthed funnel and a spoon. Fill each tin three-quarters full. Bake for 30–35 minutes. Cool until warm. Top each muffin with melted white chocolate and some berries.

"Our café has made a couple of hundred thousand of these so far, they're that delicious!"

HOT CROSS BUNS

Recipe by **SOPHIE GRAY** *from Destitute Gourmet*

MAKES: 24 | PREP TIME: 1½–1¾ HOURS | COOK TIME: 20 MINS | SKILL LEVEL: 2 (MODERATE)

INGREDIENTS

Buns

1½ cups warm water

¼ cup sweetened condensed milk

2 tbsp dried yeast granules or 1½ sachets of instant yeast

5 cups plain or high-grade flour

3 tsp mixed spice

3 tsp ground cinnamon

½ tsp salt

1 cup currants or raisins

½ cup mixed peel

50 g butter, softened

2 eggs

Crosses

1 cup plain flour

1 tsp baking powder

2 tbsp butter

about ½ cup water

Sugar glaze

3 tbsp sugar, dissolved in ⅓ cup warm water

METHOD

Blend water and condensed milk together. If using granulated yeast, sprinkle it on and stir in, then set aside for about 10 minutes until it is frothy-looking. Sift flour, spices and salt into a large bowl. If using instant yeast, add it to the dry ingredients.

Mix in the dried fruit and peel, then make a hole in the centre. Pour in the milk mixture along with the butter and eggs. Stir until combined, then turn out onto a floured surface and knead it lightly. The dough can be quite wet, so add extra flour as you knead until the dough is smooth and springy (about 10–15 minutes).

Put dough in a greased bowl and cover with greased plastic wrap. Leave in a warm place until dough doubles in size; this should take around 40 minutes.

Punch the dough down, then give it another quick knead. Divide into 24 portions and roll into balls. Place buns in a circle on a greased oven tray and cover with the greased plastic wrap from before. Leave them for around half an hour or until doubled in size.

Pre-heat the oven to 200°C. In a small bowl, blend the ingredients for the crosses, using sufficient water to make a mixture soft enough to be piped. If you haven't got a piping bag, put the mixture in a plastic bag, snip a tiny bit off the corner and squeeze the mix through. Pipe a cross pattern over the top of the buns.

Bake for 15 minutes, then brush with sugar glaze and return to the oven for a further 5 minutes, or until they look cooked.

"Hot cross buns are very much part of our culture. They are fragrant and spicy and very evocative. Enjoy!"

CHEESE MUFFINS

Recipe by **HESTER GUY** *from HG Catering*

MAKES: 6 LARGE MUFFINS | PREP TIME: 10 MINS | COOK TIME: 20–25 MINS | SKILL LEVEL: 1 (EASY)

INGREDIENTS

2 cups plain flour
4 tsp baking powder
2 tsp dry mustard
1 tsp salt
large pinch of freshly ground black pepper
2 cups grated tasty cheese
1 cup grated Parmesan cheese
¼ cup parsley, chopped
1 small red onion, chopped and sautéed
1⅓ cups milk
180 g butter, melted
2 eggs, separated

METHOD

Pre-heat oven to 200°C.

Sift dry ingredients together into a bowl, then mix in cheese and parsley.

Combine milk, butter and egg yolks.

In a separate bowl beat egg whites until soft peaks form when you lift the whisk.

Add the onion and liquid ingredients to the dry ingredients, mixing together lightly. Lastly fold in beaten egg white.

Spoon into 6 well-greased or paper-lined muffin tins. Bake for 20–25 minutes until risen and golden-brown.

TIPS

For variation, sometimes I add lots of chopped fresh herbs – chives, oregano – whatever I have, or add a good sprinkle of piri piri seasoning, which will clear everyone's sinuses at morning coffee. For a gentler spice, try 1 teaspoon of Moroccan seasoning.

This savoury mixture also marries well with chopped sun-dried tomato, or add a few chopped Kalamata olives to the mix and then press a small cube of feta into the centre of each muffin just before you cook them.

Also, muffins do not necessarily have to be baked in muffin tins – try using small flower pots which have been washed, well dried and seasoned in an oven for 20–25 minutes at 200°C. Put a small piece of tinfoil or baking paper on the base of each pot to cover the hole. Alternatively, put the mix into a lined, shallow 23 cm cake tin. Mark into wedges before cooking, and your guests can then slice themselves a piece. Presenting 'normal' food differently is a very subtle way of telling your guests you have made it yourself!

CHRISTMAS MINCE TARTS

Recipe by **LAURAINE JACOBS**

MAKES: 36 | PREP TIME: 1 HOUR | COOK TIME: 30 MINS | SKILL LEVEL: 2 (MODERATE)

INGREDIENTS

- 250 g seeded raisins
- 250 g sultanas
- 60 g candied peel
- 400 g Granny Smith apples
- 500 g currants
- 250 g brown sugar
- pinch of salt
- ¼ tsp freshly ground nutmeg
- ¼ tsp mixed spice
- juice and zest of ½ lemon
- juice and zest of ½ orange
- 3 tbsp brandy
- 250 g flaky puff or sweet shortcrust pastry
- icing sugar, for dusting

METHOD

Put raisins, sultanas and peel into a food processor. Peel and core apples, then cut into chunks and add. Process together until finely chopped but not completely pulverised. Turn out into a large bowl and add currants, sugar, salt, spices and lemon and orange juice and zest. Mix well until all is combined. Add brandy and place in well-sterilised preserving jars until needed. Makes two 950 ml jars and will keep for several months if well sealed.

Pre-heat the oven to 200°C. To make the mince tarts, roll pastry out to ½ cm thick. Using a pastry cutter, cut circles to match the size of your tart tin and ease these into the tin. Take a generous teaspoonful of the Christmas mince, smooth it into each pastry case and then cut more circles, slightly smaller, to cover the tops of the tarts. Allow the tarts to rest at room temperature for at least half an hour before cooking, then bake for about 30 minutes until the pastry is golden.

Serve warm, dusted with a little icing sugar.

"The secret to our family Christmas mince tarts is to grate Granny Smith apples into the mixture instead of suet, which makes for a lighter, delicious fruit mince. The pastry can be sweet or savoury – we make a batch of each to keep everyone happy!"

DANISH PASTRIES

Recipe by the team at **THE CLAREVILLE BAKERY**

MAKES: 18 | PREP TIME: ¾ HOUR, PLUS RISING | COOK TIME: 20 MINS | SKILL LEVEL: 3 (CHALLENGING)

INGREDIENTS

Toasted almond cream

50 g ground almonds
50 g butter
50 g caster sugar
1 egg, lightly beaten
20 g plain flour

Crème pâstissèrie (pastry creme)

250 ml milk
20 g cornflour
60 g sugar
1 egg
few drops of vanilla extract
30 g butter

To finish

1 egg, beaten
drained cherries, apricots, pears, plums or berries, halved as necessary
icing sugar, for dusting

METHOD

Prepare dough the day before using the recipe on page 18.

To prepare the toasted almond cream: pre-heat oven to 150°C. Spread ground almonds onto a baking sheet and toast for 5–8 minutes or till just changing colour. Allow to cool fully.

Beat butter with sugar till light and creamy. Beat in egg a little at a time, so as not to curdle the mixture. Add almonds and flour and mix till fully mixed in. Place in a piping bag.

Crème pâtissière: bring milk to the boil. Meanwhile, whisk cornflour and sugar together, then add egg and vanilla and whisk until smooth.

When milk has boiled, gently add it to the egg mixture while whisking briskly. Pour mixture back into the saucepan and bring back to just boiling, stirring constantly. Remove from the heat immediately and add butter, mixing really well so all the butter is incorporated. Place a layer of plastic wrap directly on the surface of crème, and refrigerate.

To finish: pre-heat oven to 220°C. Line 2 baking trays with baking paper. Remove pastry from refrigerator, divide into three and roll each piece out to a final thickness of 4–5 mm (30 cm by 20 cm for each piece). Use as little flour as possible to roll it out. Cut pastry into 10 cm squares. Pipe a ring of almond cream in the middle of each. Fold the corners into the middle and press down firmly, to prevent them popping up during baking.

Place pastries on baking trays. Cover lightly with plastic wrap and allow to rise for approximately 1–1.5 hours. Then, very gently brush with beaten egg. Press the centre of the pastry in (it will deflate slightly). Pipe in a blob of crème pâtissière and top with fruit. Bake for 20 minutes, turning trays around halfway through to make sure pastries bake evenly, until deep golden. Remove from the oven and allow to cool slightly, then transfer to a wire rack. Dust with icing sugar before serving.

PLAITED SCONES

Recipe by **DEAN BRETTSCHNEIDER**

SERVINGS: 2 (ONE SWEET, ONE SAVOURY) | PREP TIME: 25 MINS, PLUS STANDING
COOK TIME: 30–35 MINS | SKILL LEVEL: 2 (MODERATE)

INGREDIENTS

Sweet filling

100 g dates, pitted and chopped
25 ml dark rum
25 g butter, softened
1 tsp ground cinnamon

Savoury filling

75 g tasty cheese, grated
½ small egg (from below)
15 g red onion, finely chopped
1 clove garlic, crushed
15 g red capsicum, finely chopped
15 g green capsicum, finely chopped
2 tbsp fresh parlsey, finely chopped
20 g sun-dried tomatoes, finely chopped
30 g pitted olives, chopped
½ tsp smoked ground paprika

Scone dough

400 g plain flour
20 g caster sugar
25 g baking powder
good pinch of salt
70 g butter, softened
1½ eggs (use other half above)
200 ml milk
1 tbsp water
additional flour, for dusting

METHOD

Sweet filling: mix all ingredients together in a bowl, ensuring that the dates are broken down a little; cover and set aside for a few hours or overnight, then mix again. You will notice that the dates will break up easier as they soften, so the longer the soaking time the better.

Savoury filling: mix all ingredients together in a bowl to form a rough, spreadable paste. Cover and set aside until required.

Pre-heat the oven to 190–200°C.

Dough: sift flour, sugar, baking powder and salt into a large mixing bowl. Add butter and rub in, using your fingertips and thumbs, to form coarse crumbs. Whisk 1 egg and the milk together and pour into the dry ingredients. Using a wooden spoon, mix together to form a soft dough. Tip dough onto a floured surface and knead for 10–20 seconds – don't over-knead or the dough will become too elastic.

Cut dough into two equal pieces and shape into squares. Using a rolling pin, roll out each dough piece on a floured surface to a 25 cm square.

Whisk the ½ egg and water together to make an egg wash.

Evenly spread one dough square with the sweet filling and the other with the savoury filling, leaving about 1 cm free along one edge of each. Brush egg wash along that edge.

Working towards the edge painted with egg wash, firmly roll up each dough sheet to achieve a Swiss roll or log shape. Using a large chef's knife or dough scraper, make a single lengthways cut along the middle of each log, right the way through.

For each log, take one strand in each hand, with the cut side of each strand facing towards you, and twist the strands around each other. Press the ends together firmly to make sure they do not unwind during the baking process. Place the twists on a baking tray lined with baking paper, keeping them well apart so they don't join together during baking. Brush the twists with the remaining egg wash and allow them to rest for 10 minutes.

Bake for 30–35 minutes. Halfway through the baking time, turn the tray to ensure an even colour. Remove from the oven and transfer to a cooling rack.

"I always say to people, if you are interested in baking, start with scones because they are quick to master."

BAKED SPICED CUSTARD TARTS

Recipe by **SARAH & MARTIN ASPINWALL** *from Canterbury Cheesemongers*

MAKES: 12 | PREP TIME: 45 MINS | COOK TIME: 35 MINS | SKILL LEVEL: 2 (MODERATE)

INGREDIENTS

- 600 g sweet/biscuity shortcrust pastry (see p.19), at room temperature
- 1 large egg white (left over from making pastry)
- 220 ml milk
- 220 ml cream
- 85 g caster sugar
- 2 whole star anise
- 2 fresh bay leaves
- 2 large eggs
- 2 egg yolks
- 1 whole nutmeg

METHOD

Pre-heat the oven to 190°C. Spray or grease a non-stick muffin tin.

Roll pastry into a circle about 36 cm round and 4 mm thick. Use a round cutter to stamp out 12 discs of pastry to fit into the bottom of each muffin mould. Cut remaining pastry into strips wide enough to fit the sides of the muffin moulds, and gently push them into place on top of the bases to form neat tart cases within the moulds. You will need to re-roll the scraps of pastry to get enough strips to fill all the moulds. Chill in the fridge for at least 15 minutes (this prevents the pastry cases shrinking during baking).

Remove rested pastry cases from the fridge and line each one with baking paper. Add some baking beans and blind-bake for 12 minutes. Remove cases from oven and reduce the heat to 160°C. Remove baking paper and beans and brush cases well with lightly beaten egg white to seal the pastry. Put back in the oven for another 8 minutes to colour.

Meanwhile, heat milk, cream, sugar, star anise and bay leaves until nearly boiling and leave to infuse for 20 minutes. Beat whole eggs with egg yolks and stir in the infused milk mixture. Strain custard into a jug for easy pouring.

With the pastry shells still hot, fill each one with custard and grate some nutmeg onto the top. Put straight back into the oven and bake (still at 160°C) for a further 15 minutes or so. The pastry should be brown and the custard just slightly wobbly. Allow to cool before easing the tarts out of the muffin moulds.

TIPS

You can use cardamom pods or a vanilla pod instead of star anise and bay as a flavouring. And the tarts go marvellously with a chunk of cheese!

CINNAMON & WALNUT BRIOCHE

Recipe by **KIM EVANS** *from Little & Friday*

MAKES: 9 | PREP TIME: 30 MINS, PLUS DOUGH | COOK TIME: 20-30 MINS | SKILL LEVEL: 2 (MODERATE)

INGREDIENTS

1 recipe brioche dough (see p.18)
1 cup walnut halves
1 cup brown sugar
1 cup chopped dates
1 tbsp ground cinnamon
1 egg
2 tbsp milk
50 g unsalted butter

METHOD

Make brioche dough. Pre-heat the oven to 180°C. Blitz walnut halves, sugar, dates and cinnamon in a food processor, until the mixture starts resembling coarse breadcrumbs. Set aside.

On a floured surface, roll dough into a rectangle 1 cm thick. Beat egg and milk together to make egg wash and use to brush the entire dough. Spread a layer of cinnamon and walnut mix, 1 cm thick, right up to the corners of your dough. Roll up dough, rolling from the widest part. Using a sharp knife or a serrated-edge knife, slice pieces 5 cm thick.

Grease large muffin tins with baking spray or butter. Place the scrolls into the tins, cut side up. Brush with egg wash. Bake for 20 minutes or until golden-brown. Cool before removing from tins.

BAKLAVA

Recipe by the team at **DIMITRIS GREEK FOOD**

MAKES: 30–45 | PREP TIME: 25 MINS | COOK TIME: 20–25 MINS | SKILL LEVEL: 2 (MODERATE)

INGREDIENTS

Baklava

1 cup shelled pistachios
2 cups almonds
2 cups walnuts
1½ cups sugar
1½ tbsp ground cinnamon
1 x 375 g packet filo pastry
melted butter, for layering
whole cloves

Syrup

2 cups sugar
2 cups water
juice and zest of 2 lemons
2–3 cinnamon quills
1 heaped tbsp ground cloves

METHOD

Pre-heat the oven to 180°C regular bake.

Place pistachios, almonds, walnuts, sugar and cinnamon in a large food processor and process into a fine crumb.

Brush two to three sheets of filo with butter and layer them. On the top layer of filo apply a thin layer of melted butter, then add a layer of nut crumb mixture over the first two-thirds of the filo. Beginning at the nut-covered end, roll up the filo tightly into a cylinder and place on a baking tray. Repeat until all the nut mixture is used.

Cut the cylinders into your desired length, and place a whole clove at the centre of every piece. Place the tray into the middle of your oven and cook until golden, about 20 minutes.

While the baklava is cooking, prepare the syrup. Place all ingredients in a saucepan and simmer over a medium heat for about 10 minutes.

When the baklava is ready, pour the warm syrup over it while it is still hot. Spoon any excess syrup over the baklava until all the syrup is absorbed.

TIPS

Sprinkle the cut ends of your baklava with water to prevent it drying out too quickly during the baking process.

Prick the baklava with a fork before baking, to help the syrup seep into it.

CARROT & ZUCCHINI MUFFINS

Recipe by **JOSH EMETT**

MAKES: 6 LARGE OR 12 STANDARD MUFFINS | PREP TIME: 15 MINS
COOK TIME: 15–25 MINS | SKILL LEVEL: 1 (EASY)

INGREDIENTS

250 g caster sugar
250 ml oil
170 g eggs (approx. 3)
265 g plain flour
1 tsp mixed spice
1 tsp bicarbonate of soda
2 tsp baking powder
pinch of salt
200 g grated carrot
(2 medium-sized carrots)
200 g grated zucchini
(2 medium-sized zucchini)
100 g sultanas or raisins
3 tbsp wholegrain oats

DF

METHOD

Pre-heat the oven to 210°C. Grease the holes of a standard or large muffin tin.

Beat the sugar, oil and eggs together until the sugar is dissolved, then fold in the flour, mixed spice, bicarbonate of soda, baking powder and salt. Finally, mix in the carrot, zucchini and sultanas or raisins.

Two-thirds fill the muffin tins and sprinkle oats on top. Bake for around 15 minutes (standard muffins) or 25 minutes (large muffins). Cool in the tin for a few minutes before removing to a wire rack.

CARAMELISED ONION & CHEDDAR SCONES

Recipe by the team at **BOSCO CAFÉ**

MAKES: 16 | PREP TIME: 20 MINS | COOK TIME: 15 MINS | SKILL LEVEL: 1 (EASY)

INGREDIENTS

6 onions
4 tbsp oil, for cooking
6 cups flour
2 tbsp baking powder
2 tsp salt
4 tsp caster sugar
6 cups grated tasty cheese
600 ml milk (approx.)
extra milk and grated tasty cheese, for topping

METHOD

Pre-heat the oven to 180°C on fan-bake. Finely slice onions and sauté in oil until soft and caramelised, stirring as needed to prevent them sticking to the pan.

Sift flour, baking powder and salt together and add sugar. Stir in cheese and add milk. Mix well to combine, adding a little more milk if necessary. Turn out onto a floured surface and shape into a rectangle. Cut in half, and roll each half to form two even squares, about 1 cm thick.

Spread one square with caramelised onion. Carefully lift the other square and place on top. Cut into 16 even-sized pieces. Place on baking trays and brush with milk. Sprinkle with a little grated cheese. Bake for approximately 15 minutes, until golden-brown and not too soft to the touch.

"These scones come out of the oven around 8:20 every morning, and there's a bit of a rush in the café as the scone lovers come in."

PLAIN & DATE SCONES

Recipe by **PETA MATHIAS**

MAKES: 12 | PREP TIME: 10 MINS | COOK TIME: 10 MINS | SKILL LEVEL: 1 (EASY)

INGREDIENTS

- 4 cups flour
- 4 heaped tsp baking powder
- ½ tsp salt
- 4 tbsp butter, cubed
- 1 cup chopped dates (optional)
- 2 cups buttermilk

METHOD

Pre-heat the oven to 220°C, and grease a baking tray or use a non-stick baking sheet.

Sift the flour, baking powder and salt into a bowl. Rub the butter in with your fingertips or cut it in with two knives. If using dates, stir them in. Mix in the buttermilk with your hands or a knife.

Turn the wet dough out onto the bench and knead lightly for a few seconds. Press or roll out to 3 cm thick, then cut into squares about 5 cm x 5 cm.

Whip them into the oven for 10 minutes. Serve immediately with jam and cream.

"When we were children my father used to leave Mass early on Sunday to go home and make these scones. When we got home from church we could smell them coming out of the oven. We had been fasting so we were practically fainting as we came in the door."

REFRIGERATOR MUFFINS

Recipe by **HESTER GUY** *from HG Catering*

MAKES: 14 LARGE MUFFINS (4–5 BATCHES) | PREP TIME: 10 MINS | COOK TIME: 20–30 MINS | SKILL LEVEL: 1 (EASY)

INGREDIENTS

Base mix (enough for 4–5 batches)

2 cups All Bran

2½ cups sultanas

3 cups boiling water

1 tbsp baking soda

1 tsp salt

4 cups plain flour

2 cups dark cane sugar or brown sugar

1½ cups chopped nuts, e.g. freshly shelled walnuts, lightly browned almonds or Brazil nuts

1 cup wheatgerm

4 cups bran flakes

4 eggs

1 cup salad oil (canola)

Additions – to every 3 cups of base mix add:

1 apple, skin on, grated

½–1 cup frozen blueberries

1 tbsp chia seeds

Optional topping

1 tbsp dark cane sugar

1 tbsp sesame seeds

DF

METHOD

Place All Bran and sultanas in a bowl and pour boiling water over. Allow to cool.

Sift baking soda, salt and flour together. Add sugar and nuts, and mix. Add wheatgerm and bran flakes and combine thoroughly. Make a well in the centre of the dry ingredients.

Combine eggs, oil and the All Bran and sultana mix, and pour into the well in the centre of the dry ingredients. Mix together lightly. Store in the refrigerator for up to seven days.

To use: pre-heat oven to 170°C. Take 3 cups of the base mixture. Add grated apple, frozen blueberries and chia seeds. Mix together lightly.

Place muffin papers in large muffin pans, and fill papers nearly to the top as these muffins do not rise. If you wish, dust with cane sugar (I like the sweetness) and sprinkle with sesame seeds. Alternatively, you could top with extra blueberries and chia seeds. Bake for 20–30 minutes or until golden-brown.

"Jo, a dear friend of mine, used to make these refrigerator muffins for her children's school lunches. Very healthy! The basic mix keeps in the fridge for a week."

ECCLES CAKES

Recipe by **SARAH & MARTIN ASPINWALL** *from Canterbury Cheesemongers*

MAKES: 8 | PREP TIME: 45 MINS | COOK TIME: 20–30 MINS | SKILL LEVEL: 2 (MODERATE)

INGREDIENTS

250 g currants
100 g caster sugar
40 g butter, melted
1 level tsp freshly ground nutmeg
1 level tsp ground ginger
1 level tsp allspice
600 g rough puff pastry, chilled (see p.19)
1 egg
a little milk

METHOD

Pre-heat the oven to 180–190°C. In a bowl, mix together currants, 70 grams of sugar, butter and spices. Let them sit for at least 15 minutes for the flavours to combine.

Divide your pastry into eight equal pieces, and on a floured surface roll each into a 12 cm square. Mix egg with milk to make an egg wash, and brush this on the outer edges of each square. Place a tablespoonful of currant mixture in the centre of each square. Gather up the edges and crimp together to form a cross-shaped seal.

Turn your Eccles cakes over and gently round the ends so they become more of an oval shape. Place them on a baking sheet lined with baking paper, brush with egg wash and sprinkle with remaining caster sugar. Use some scissors or a sharp knife to make three small cuts on top to let the steam out when cooking.

Chill for a minimum of 15 minutes in the fridge or a cool place, to allow time for the pastry to relax. Bake for 20–30 minutes or until golden and cooked. Remove to a rack to cool.

TIP

Eccles cakes go really well with chunks of cheese for morning tea or dessert – the savoury and sweet make a wonderful combination.

BANANA, PINEAPPLE & PECAN MUFFINS

Recipe by **CAZNA GILDER** *from Mrs Clark's Cafe*

MAKES: 6–7 LARGE OR 12 STANDARD MUFFINS | PREP TIME: 15 MINS | COOK TIME: 15–30 MINS | SKILL LEVEL: 1 (EASY)

INGREDIENTS

Muffins

2 black bananas, smashed
½ tin crushed pineapple
2 eggs
½ cup plain unsweetened yoghurt
1 cup milk
50 g butter, melted
2¾ cups plain flour
3 tsp baking powder
½ tsp ground cinnamon
pinch of salt
¼ cup sugar

Topping

¼ cup sugar
1 tbsp ground cinnamon
whole pecans, as needed

METHOD

Pre-heat oven to 190°C. Grease the holes of a standard or large muffin tin, or line with paper cases.

Beat banana, pineapple, eggs, yoghurt, milk and butter together.

Sift flour, baking powder, cinnamon and salt together into a separate, large bowl. Add sugar and stir to mix.

Pour wet ingredients into dry, and fold together gently until just combined. Spoon into muffin tin. Top with pecans (one per standard muffin and three per large muffin).

Mix sugar and cinnamon together and sprinkle over each muffin.

Bake for 15 minutes (standard muffins) or 25–30 minutes (large mwuffins). Cool on a wire rack.

NADIA LIM

NOT-SO-NAUGHTY

RAW BERRY ICE CREAM CAKE

Recipe by **NADIA LIM**

SERVINGS: 8 | PREP TIME: 20 MINS, PLUS FREEZING | COOK TIME: 40 MINS | SKILL LEVEL: 1 (EASY)

INGREDIENTS

Base

¾ cup desiccated or shredded coconut

120 g Medjool dates, stone removed (or 15–16 ordinary dried dates soaked in boiling water for 5 minutes)

⅓ cup sunflower seeds (or pumpkin seeds, rolled oats, almonds, hazelnuts or macadamias)

50 g coconut oil (or butter), melted

Filling

500 g frozen raspberries (or strawberries, boysenberries, blackberries or a mixture of berries)

3–4 tbsp pure maple syrup, or liquid honey (not mānuka as it has too strong a flavour) or agave syrup

½ cup coconut cream (or cream)

2 egg whites (can be left out if necessary)

To garnish

fresh strawberries or other berries, sliced

DF GF

METHOD

Grease a 20–21 cm round spring-form cake tin and line the bottom and sides with baking paper.

For the base: place all the base ingredients in a food processor and blitz until well combined and the mixture has formed a slightly sticky dough. Scrape down the sides of the food processor as necessary, to ensure all the ingredients are incorporated. Press mixture into the base of the prepared tin using the back of a wet spoon. Place in the freezer while you make the filling.

For the filling: place frozen berries in the food processor and blitz until crumbly. Add syrup/honey and coconut cream (or cream) and continue blitzing until the mixture is the consistency of sorbet or ice cream, scraping down the sides of the food processor as necessary. Add egg whites and continue blitzing for 1–2 more minutes; the mixture will become light, fluffy, smooth and ice cream-like, and a paler pink colour.

Spoon filling on top of base and roughly smooth out the top. Return to the freezer immediately. Leave for at least 6 hours (or overnight), until set.

To serve: when ready to serve, remove from freezer and stand at room temperature for 10 minutes to thaw slightly. Garnish with sliced fresh strawberries. Use a large, sharp knife to cut slices of cake.

"This amazing cake is refined sugar-free, gluten-free and nut-free, and has the option of being dairy-free too. It tastes like you're eating sorbet, ice cream and cookie base in cake form! For me, this is the perfect summer dessert."

CHOCOLATE, ORANGE & FIG BUCKWHEAT BARS

Recipe by **OLIVIA SCOTT** *from The Raw Kitchen*

MAKES: 12 | PREP TIME: 10 MINS, PLUS SOAKING | SKILL LEVEL: 1 (EASY)

INGREDIENTS

2 cups buckwheat
1 cup almonds
½ cup cacao powder
5 fresh or dried figs, sliced
2 scoops protein powder
5 tbsp coconut oil
zest and juice of 1 orange
½ tsp vanilla bean powder or paste
½ tsp Himalayan sea salt

(DF) (GF)

METHOD

The night before, place buckwheat in a bowl, cover with cold water and leave to soak for 8 hours.

Line a 15–20 cm rectangular or square baking tin with baking paper.

Place buckwheat and almonds in a food processor, and blend lightly so that the mixture combines and breaks down. Add remaining ingredients, and blend further until consistency is sticky and is able to be moulded with your hands.

Press mixture flat into the lined tin. Place in the refrigerator for 1 hour to set, then turn out and slice into rectangular bars. Store refrigerated in an airtight container for up to three weeks.

"Sweeten these bars with your favourite protein powder to give them an extra boost! I love to throw some vanilla pea protein in and have them after the gym, or as a mid-morning energy snack."

CARAMEL NUT BUTTER BISCUITS

Recipe by **ELEANOR OZICH** *from Petite Kitchen*

MAKES: 10 | PREP TIME: 10 MINS | COOK TIME: 7–10 MINS | SKILL LEVEL: 1 (EASY)

INGREDIENTS

1 cup (270 g) nut butter (e.g. almond butter)

½ cup (75 g) coconut sugar or rapadura (unrefined cane) sugar

1 large egg

(DF) (GF)

METHOD

Pre-heat oven to 180°C, and line a baking tray with baking paper.

Add all ingredients to a mixing bowl. Mix until well combined – the mixture will be a little sticky, but don't worry.

Using damp hands, roll into small balls about the size of a golf ball and place 2–3 cm apart on the baking tray. Press down gently with a fork. Bake for 6–7 minutes (some ovens might need a little longer).

Cool on a wire rack. Will keep for up to a week in an airtight container.

"The best things in life are simple, like these gorgeous three-ingredient caramel nut butter biscuits."

RAW RASPBERRY BROWNIE

Recipe by **MEGAN MAY** *from Little Bird*

SERVINGS: 6 | PREP TIME: 10 MINS | COOK TIME: 40 MINS | SKILL LEVEL: 1 (EASY)

INGREDIENTS

- 2 cups Brazil nuts
- 2½ cups pitted dates
- 1 tsp sea salt
- 2 tsp vanilla extract
- 1½ avocados, pitted and peeled
- ¾ cup raw cacao powder or good-quality organic cocoa powder
- 3 tbsp melted coconut oil or cacao butter
- ¼ cup freeze-dried raspberries or ½ cup fresh or frozen raspberries

DF GF

METHOD

Pulse Brazil nuts in a food processor until slightly chunky, then add dates, salt, vanilla, avocado, cacao/cocoa powder and coconut oil or cacao butter. Pulse for approximately 30 seconds, until the mixture comes together well but there is still texture to it.

Add two-thirds of the raspberries and pulse them in.

Line a baking tray approximately 12 cm x 20 cm with plastic wrap or baking paper and press the mixture in. Top with the remaining raspberries, cover and leave to set in the fridge for 2 hours or the freezer for 1 hour.

Cut into 6–8 squares. Enjoy! It will keep in the fridge for a week or in the freezer for one month.

TIPS

When serving, be aware that it will soften at room temperature. If you're taking it to a friend's place, transport it in a cooler bag or put in the fridge when you get there.

If you can't get freeze-dried raspberries, use fresh or frozen raspberries instead; just increase the amount to half a cup (freeze-dried products always have a more concentrated flavour). You will need to store the brownie in the freezer if you are using fresh or frozen raspberries, as otherwise it will have a very short shelf-life – which is fine if you are going to eat it straight away.

> ***"Raw foods generally make people feel a lot better and more energized – and who doesn't want that?"***

BEETROOT CHOCOLATE LOAF CAKE

Recipe by **NIKI BEZZANT** *from Healthy Food Guide*

SERVINGS: 4 | PREP TIME: 20 MINS | COOK TIME: 40–50 MINS | SKILL LEVEL: 1 (EASY)

INGREDIENTS

3 large beetroots (enough to make 3 cups when grated)

4 eggs

⅛ cup oil (we use grapeseed)

¾ cup date syrup (see tip adjacent)

2 tsp vanilla extract

1 tsp baking soda

pinch of salt

1 tsp ground cinnamon

½ cup good-quality cocoa powder

¼ cup ground almonds

¼ cup coconut flour

(DF) (GF)

METHOD

Pre-heat oven to 170°C. Line a 20 cm x 10 cm loaf tin with baking paper.

Place beetroot in a microwave-proof bowl, cover and microwave on high for 6–8 minutes until tender. Set aside for 3–5 minutes, until cool enough to handle, then grate (use gloves to protect hands from staining).

Combine beetroot, eggs and oil in a large bowl and beat together using a hand-mixer. Add date syrup, vanilla, baking soda, salt and cinnamon. Beat until well combined and smooth. Add cocoa, almonds and coconut flour and stir through until well combined.

Pour into prepared tin. Bake for 30–40 minutes until a skewer inserted into the centre comes out clean. Cool in tin before turning out.

TIP

To make date syrup, combine 1 cup of dates and 1 cup of water in a pot and bring to the boil. Simmer gently for 5 minutes, then cool. Place cooled mixture in a blender or foodprocessor and purée until smooth. Use in place of sugar or syrup, in roughly similar weights. This syrup can be stored in the fridge or freezer.

"Who'd have thought the humble beetroot would be the mystery ingredient in this dense, dark cake? Most people won't be able to pick it, but it's fun asking them to guess!"

RAW BLUEBERRY CHEESECAKE SLICE

Recipe by **JOCELYN HUGHES** *from Ripe Delicatessen*

MAKES: 20 SLICES | PREP TIME: 25 MINS, PLUS OVERNIGHT | SKILL LEVEL: 1 (EASY)

INGREDIENTS

Base

¾ cup (100 g) raw cashews
1 cup (100 g) ground almonds
½ cup (70 g) raisins
2 cups (160 g) desiccated coconut
3 tbsp coconut oil, melted

Topping

¼ cup (35 g) raw cashews
6 tbsp (90 ml) lemon juice
2 tbsp almond butter
2 tbsp coconut cream
½ cup maple syrup
½ cup (70 g) frozen blueberries, defrosted
½ tsp vanilla extract
½ cup coconut oil, melted
1 tbsp freeze-dried blueberries (optional)

(DF) (GF)

METHOD

Grease a 20 cm x 30 cm slice tin and line with baking paper.

For the base: place the cashews in a food processor. Pulse in bursts until they turn into a fine, sandy, flour-like consistency, scraping the sides and bottom of the bowl often. Watch it – don't let it turn into nut butter!

When ready, add the ground almonds and pulse to combine. Add the raisins and pulse until lightly blended. Add the coconut and pulse again. Lastly, add the coconut oil, blending until well combined. Press the mixture into the prepared tin in an even layer. Place in the refrigerator for 10 minutes to firm up.

For the topping: place the cashews in the food processor. Pulse in bursts until the nuts turn into a fine, sandy, flour-like consistency. Add all the remaining ingredients except the coconut oil and blueberries, and pulse again until incorporated. Add the coconut oil and blend until well combined.

Pour the mixture over the base, and sprinkle with freeze-dried blueberries, if using. Place in the refrigerator overnight to set. Once set, it will keep for four to five days in the refrigerator in an airtight container. Cut into slices when ready to serve. This slice freezes well – defrost overnight in the refrigerator.

RAW CHOCOLATE COCONUT BARS

Recipe by **HANNAH HORTON** *from Mondays Wholefoods*

MAKES: ABOUT 16 | PREP TIME: 15 MINS, PLUS FREEZING | SKILL LEVEL: 1 (EASY)

INGREDIENTS

Filling

2 cups desiccated coconut

1 cup full-fat coconut cream

¼ cup coconut oil, melted

4 tbsp natural liquid sweetener (pure maple syrup, coconut syrup or rice malt syrup)

1 tsp vanilla extract

pinch of sea salt

Chocolate coating

1 cup coconut oil, softened

⅓ cup cocoa or raw cacao powder

1–2 tbsp natural liquid sweetener (see options above)

(DF) (GF)

METHOD

Combine all filling ingredients in a bowl and mix very well. Spoon this mixture into a rectangular container lined with baking paper and press down firmly. Place the container in the freezer and let it cool completely.

When very firm, remove from the freezer and cut into bars. Return to the freezer, as you want the bars to be very cold when you dip them in chocolate. Now you can prepare the chocolate coating by placing the coconut oil, cocoa/cacao powder and sweetener into a blender and combining until smooth, glossy and a little bit runny, like warm honey. Pour the chocolate into a 500 ml measuring cup or similar.

Remove the coconut bars from the freezer and, one by one, dip an end into the chocolate and place the bar on baking paper. By the time you've dipped them all, the chocolate should have hardened on the first ones, so go back and dip the other end. Repeat this process until your bars are completely covered in a nice thick layer of chocolate.

And that's it! They are ready to enjoy straight away, or pop them in the fridge or freezer for the perfect anytime snack – if they last that long!

"This recipe is proof that eating well does not mean missing out on the best things in life. These little beauties are so addictive and inspired by my all time favourite Bounty Bar."

KIWIFRUIT CASHEW MOUSSE CAKE

Recipe by **STEPHEN BARRY** *from Mount Bistro*

SERVINGS: 4 | PREP TIME: 25 MINS, PLUS SETTING | SKILL LEVEL: 1 (EASY)

INGREDIENTS

Base

⅔ cup macadamia meal
3 fresh dates, pitted

Filling

4 gold kiwifruit, peeled
½ cup cashews
¼ cup maple syrup
1 tsp lime zest
½ cup coconut oil

Crumble topping

½ cup chopped macadamia nuts
½ cup shaved coconut
1 tbsp maple syrup
1 tbsp coconut oil

(DF) (GF)

METHOD

Grease four 6 cm stainless-steel food rings and place on a baking tray lined with baking paper. Put macadamia meal and dates in a food processor and pulse until combined. Spoon crust mixture into the rings and press firmly into the pan with a coffee tamper or small spice jar wrapped in baking paper or plastic wrap so that the base doesn't stick to it. Set aside.

Place 2 kiwifruit in a food processor and purée on slow speed. Pass the purée through a sieve to remove the seeds. Return kiwifruit pulp to the processor, adding cashews, maple syrup and lime zest. Blend for a little while, then add coconut oil and continue to blend until everything is well combined and the batter is nice and smooth. Spoon the fruit filling on top of the base, then place in the fridge and let it set for a few hours.

To make the crumble topping, pre-heat oven to 170°C. Combine macadamia nuts, coconut, maple syrup and coconut oil. Place on a tray and toast in the oven until golden, about 6 minutes – keep an eye on it. Cool.

Peel and dice remaining kiwifruit. Remove mousses from the fridge, top with a layer of diced kiwifruit and then a layer of crumble mix; remove the ring and serve. I serve them with a splatter of coconut cream flavoured with a little lime zest and vanilla paste.

TIPS

When puréeing kiwifruit, use a slow speed so you don't crack the seeds – cracked seeds can have a bitter taste.

If you are into raw food, use a dehydrator to 'toast' the nuts for the crumble.

APRICOT, GINGER & PISTACHIO BALLS IN TOASTED COCONUT

Recipe by **PETER GORDON**

MAKES: ABOUT 18 | PREP TIME: 20 MINS | SKILL LEVEL: 1 (EASY)

INGREDIENTS

200 g long-thread desiccated coconut

300 g dried apricots, halved

50 g crystallised ginger

150 g condensed milk

100 g pistachios, chopped roughly

GF

METHOD

Pre-heat oven to 160°C.

Place coconut in a baking dish and toast in oven until golden, stirring several times – about 8–10 minutes, depending on the thickness of your coconut. Cool.

Pulse-blitz apricots and ginger in a food processor until you get smallish pieces. Add condensed milk and briefly blitz – don't overwork it.

Tip onto your bench and flatten out to ½ cm thick. Sprinkle pistachios over, then gently knead together until combined.

Dampen your hands in cold water, then roll the paste into balls and toss in the coconut, pressing it on to coat them. Keep in the fridge, covered tightly, for up to two weeks.

"We'd make a version of these in Whanganui which was much simpler, but as my tastes have changed the addition of ginger and pistachios makes them that little more interesting. Would my younger self have approved of their fancy new get-up? Hell, yeah!"

ASPARAGUS, MINT & FETA BREAD

Recipe by **ELEANOR OZICH** *from Petite Kitchen*

SERVINGS: 8 | PREP TIME: 15 MINS | COOK TIME: 45–50 MINS | SKILL LEVEL: 1 (EASY)

INGREDIENTS

1 bunch asparagus
1 tbsp oil, for cooking
1 onion, chopped finely
1 cup (40 g) finely chopped spinach
1 cup (140 g) spelt flour, or flour of your choice
5 free-range eggs
1 cup (75 g) grated Cheddar cheese
¼ cup olive oil
handful of fresh mint, sliced finely
1 tsp sea salt
½ tsp ground pepper
¼ cup (50 g) feta, crumbled
olive oil, for drizzling

METHOD

Pre-heat the oven to 180°C. Line a loaf tin with baking paper, allowing the sides to over hang.

Trim the hard ends off the asparagus and blanch in boiling water for about 1 minute. Remove and set aside to cool.

Heat the oil in a frying pan and gently sauté the onion until soft. Allow to cool a little. Combine the onion, spinach, flour, eggs, cheese, olive oil, mint, salt and pepper in a large bowl. Mix until well incorporated, and then transfer to the lined loaf tin. Place the asparagus spears lengthwise on top, then sprinkle with feta. Drizzle with a little olive oil.

Bake for 45 minutes, or until a skewer comes out clean when inserted into the centre. Leave to cool in the tin for 15 minutes or so before carefully turning out onto a cooling rack.

Slice thickly. Best enjoyed on the day of making, although it freezes and toasts well.

"This simple rustic-style bread is absolutely packed full of flavour. We like to enjoy thick slices with a mug of tea."

NOT-SO-NAUGHTY

HAZELNUT & APRICOT FRUIT & NUT BARS

Recipe by **MEGAN MAY** *from Little Bird*

MAKES: 12 SMALL OR 6 LARGE BARS | PREP TIME: 15 MINS, PLUS SETTING | SKILL LEVEL: 1 (EASY)

INGREDIENTS

½ cup gluten-free oats
¼ cup almond butter
¾ cup Medjool or other soft dates, pitted
⅓ cup cacao powder
½ tsp vanilla extract
pinch of salt
¼ cup coconut oil
¼ cup dried apricots (sulphur-free), diced
2 tbsp cacao nibs
½ cup hazelnuts (activated and dried, or roasted lightly)

(DF) (GF)

METHOD

Blend oats into a fine flour-like consistency in a food processor, then add almond butter and dates and blend until mixture becomes slightly sticky. Now add cacao, vanilla, salt and coconut oil and blend until it comes together.

Add apricots, cacao nibs and half the hazelnuts to the food processor and pulse until the hazelnuts have been lightly crushed.

This mixture will be firm and easy to work with. Take a piece of baking paper and use it to line a small slice tin. Then take the mixture out of the food processor and shape it with your hands into a 12 cm x 18 cm slab that's about 1 cm high. Press remaining hazelnuts into the top of the slab.

Place in the fridge for 1 hour to set, then remove and slice into 6 or 12 bars. Store in an airtight container in the fridge.

"This is an ode to the classic fruit and nut chocolate bar you might get at the supermarket. It's ridiculously easy to make and in around 15 minutes you can whip up a batch that will last a few weeks."

NOT-SO-NAUGHTY

BANANA & SULTANA BREAD

Recipe by **NIKI BEZZANT** *from Healthy Food Guide*

SERVINGS: 14 | PREP TIME: 10 MINS, PLUS CHILLING | COOK TIME: 30–40 MINS | SKILL LEVEL: 1 (EASY)

INGREDIENTS

¼ cup (50 g) sultanas
2 tsp vanilla extract
¼ cup boiling water
1 cup gluten-free baking mix
1 cup ground almonds
¼ cup shredded coconut
¼ cup (30 g) walnuts, chopped roughly
1 tsp ground cinnamon
2 ripe bananas, mashed
3 eggs
4 tbsp peanut butter

(DF) (GF)

METHOD

Pre-heat oven to 180°C. Line a 20 cm x 10 cm loaf tin with baking paper.

Mix together sultanas, vanilla and boiling water in a jug. Set aside.

In a large bowl, combine baking mix, ground almonds, coconut, walnuts and cinnamon.

Place bananas, eggs and peanut butter in a separate bowl. Mix well. Add to dry ingredients. Add sultana mixture and stir to combine.

Spoon mixture into loaf tin. Bake for 30 minutes, or until golden on top. Cool in tin before turning out.

TIP

I like to slice up the loaf once it's cooled and store slices in the freezer, ready to toast and top with peanut butter for a mid-afternoon snack.

"This loaf has no added sugar – the sweetness comes naturally from the banana and sultanas."

NOT-SO-NAUGHTY

FRUIT & NUT RAW CHOCOLATE

Recipe by **OLIVIA SCOTT** *from The Raw Kitchen*

MAKES: 1 BLOCK | PREP TIME: 5 MINS, PLUS CHILLING | SKILL LEVEL: 1 (EASY)

INGREDIENTS

2 cups coconut oil, softened to liquid
½ cup maple syrup
1 cup cacao powder
1 tsp vanilla bean powder or paste
½ tsp Himalayan sea salt
1 tsp ground cinnamon

Garnish

2 tbsp pumpkin seeds
4 tbsp pistachios, chopped
3 tbsp freeze-dried raspberries

DF GF

METHOD

Line a baking tray with baking paper.

Place coconut oil in a bowl and stir in maple syrup and cacao powder. Add vanilla bean powder or paste, salt and cinnamon, using a fork to ensure that there are no lumps. Once smooth, pour into lined baking tray. Sprinkle with pumpkin seeds, pistachio and raspberries. Place in the refrigerator for 30 minutes to set.

To serve, use a large knife to cut into squares, or break apart with your fingers. Store refrigerated in an airtight container for up to one month.

TIP

If you cannot source freeze-dried raspberries, replace them with goji berries, dried blueberries or sultanas.

"I love making this if I have friends coming over for dinner and need to whip up a last-minute after-dinner treat."

NOT-SO-NAUGHTY

CITRUS, ROSEMARY & HONEY POLENTA CAKE

Recipe by **NADIA LIM**

SERVINGS: 10 | PREP TIME: 15 MINS | COOK TIME: ABOUT 1 HOUR | SKILL LEVEL: 1 (EASY)

INGREDIENTS

Cake

125 g butter, softened

1 tsp vanilla extract

zest of 2 oranges, grated finely

zest of 2 lemons, grated finely

1½–2 tsp very finely chopped rosemary leaves

3 free-range eggs

⅓ cup natural unsweetened yoghurt, plus extra to serve

¾ cup liquid honey

½ cup freshly squeezed orange juice

½ cup freshly squeezed lemon juice

1 cup fine polenta

1 cup ground almonds

1½ tsp gluten-free baking powder

Orange and rosemary syrup

zest of 1 orange, cut into very thin strips (use a vegetable peeler)

1½ cups freshly squeezed orange juice

2 tbsp liquid honey

1 sprig rosemary

GF

METHOD

Pre-heat oven to 160°C. Grease and line a 22 cm round spring-form cake tin with baking paper.

In a large mixing bowl, cream butter, vanilla, orange zest, lemon zest and rosemary together.

In a separate bowl, whisk eggs and yoghurt together until smooth. Add to creamed mixture, along with honey, and whisk until smooth and well combined. Add orange and lemon juice to mixture, along with polenta, ground almonds and baking powder, and whisk until all the ingredients are well combined and you have a nice smooth batter.

Pour into the prepared cake tin and bake for about 60–65 minutes, or until a skewer inserted in the middle of the cake comes out clean. Leave in the tin to cool slightly while you make the syrup.

To make the syrup, boil all the ingredients in a small pot for about 5 minutes, until the liquid is reduced by about a third. Pour all over the cake in the tin, while it is still warm. Leave to stand for at least 10 minutes (for the syrup to soak in) before removing cake from tin. Serve warm or cold, with yoghurt.

TIP

If you have a food processor, simply place all the cake ingredients in it and pulse a few times until the batter is smooth and well combined, then pour into your prepared cake tin.

"This cake is gluten-free and refined sugar-free, and bursts with zesty flavour."

COCONUT ALMOND POWER BARS

Recipe by **MICHAEL VAN DE ELZEN**

MAKES: 12 LARGE OR 24 SMALL BARS | PREP TIME: 10 MINS, PLUS COOLING
COOK TIME: 30 MINS | SKILL LEVEL: 1 (EASY)

INGREDIENTS

- 2½ cups (280 g) cooking oats
- ½ cup (45 g) shredded coconut
- ½ tsp sea salt
- ½ tsp ground cinnamon
- ½ cup (80 g) chopped dried apricots
- 2 tbsp almond butter
- 100 g good-quality dark cooking chocolate
- ½ cup raw honey
- 1 tsp vanilla paste

METHOD

Pre-heat oven to 160°C and line a 20 cm x 30cm baking tray with baking paper.

Mix oats, coconut, salt, cinnamon and apricots in a large bowl. Place almond butter, chocolate and honey in a heavy-based saucepan over a low heat. Stir until melted together. Stir in vanilla paste, then pour over the dry mix and work quickly to combine. Press into baking tray and put in oven for 30 minutes.

Remove from oven and allow to cool completely (finishing in the fridge), before cutting into bars.

"Get your kids involved in making these beauties and before you know it they'll be baking their own school lunches!"

SAVOURY BREAKFAST TART

Recipe by **AMY MELCHIOR** *from Ripe Delicatessen*

SERVINGS: 6–8 | PREP TIME: 25 MINS | COOK TIME: 25–30 MINS | SKILL LEVEL: 1 (EASY)

INGREDIENTS

Base

1½ cups (150 g) ground almonds

¾ cup (90 g) coconut flour

1 tbsp chia seeds

pinch of sea salt

1 tsp smoked paprika

1 egg

6 tbsp coconut oil, melted

Filling

4 free-range eggs

¼ tsp sea salt

¼ tsp freshly ground black pepper

½ small red onion, finely diced

2 courgettes, grated

3 rashers (90 g) streaky bacon, cooked and diced (optional)

½ cup (20 g) finely chopped spinach

¼ cup (15 g) finely chopped parsley

DF GF

METHOD

Pre-heat oven to 180°C. Grease a 36 cm x 13 cm rectangular tart tin or a 26 cm round tart tin.

Base: place all the ingredients in a food processor bowl and blend until well combined, scraping down the walls of the bowl a couple of times.

Place the mix into the base of the tart tin and push it firmly into the tin so that some of the mix lines the sides. Using a fork, pick the base to allow steam to escape. Place in the oven to bake for 10 minutes or until golden and firm. Remove from the oven and set aside to cool a little.

Filling: in a medium-sized mixing bowl, whisk the eggs and seasoning together. Add all the remaining ingredients and mix until combined. Spoon the mix into the tart tin and bake for 15–20 minutes or until the egg is just cooked through.

Remove from the oven and set aside to cool a little before removing from the tin.

CARDAMOM-SPICED CHIA SEED PUDDING

Recipe by **HANNAH HORTON** *from Mondays Wholefoods*

SERVINGS: 2–4 | PREP TIME: 20 MINS | SKILL LEVEL: 1 (EASY)

INGREDIENTS

Chia seed mix

4 tbsp white chia seeds
250 ml coconut water
1 tsp vanilla extract
½ tsp ground cinnamon
¼ tsp ground cardamom
¼ cup coconut chips

Assembly

coconut yoghurt (you can substitute with regular unsweetened Greek yoghurt)
1 fresh mango, cut into thin slices
2 passionfruit, pulped
1 lime, sliced finely
edible flowers, to garnish

(DF) (GF)

METHOD

Combine all chia seed mix ingredients in a bowl and set aside until the chia seeds have fully hydrated and the mixture is thick (this usually takes about 15 minutes).

Spoon half of the chia mixture into two medium-sized glass bowls or four smaller glass cups. Place a generous layer of mango on top of the chia mix. Spoon a thick layer of coconut yoghurt (or regular yoghurt) on top of that, followed by passionfruit, and then the remaining chia mix.

Decorate with mango and lime slices, and edible flowers. Enjoy!

"This dish is so simple to prepare and perfect at any time of day, from breakfast to dessert! What's more, you can switch out the fruit to suit the season – the flavours are always great."

CHEWY CASHEW, GINGER & HONEY COOKIES

Recipe by **OLIVIA SCOTT** *from The Raw Kitchen*

MAKES: 10–12 | PREP TIME: 10 MINS | COOK TIME: 8 HOURS | SKILL LEVEL: 1 (EASY)

INGREDIENTS

½ cup honey
2 cups cashew nuts
1 tbsp ground ginger powder
½ cup pumpkin seeds
½ cup sunflower seeds
¼ cup white sesame seeds
¼ cup black sesame seeds
¼ cup goji berries
½ tsp vanilla bean powder or paste
½ tsp Himalayan sea salt
3 tbsp coconut oil

(DF) (GF)

METHOD

Beforehand, place honey in refrigerator to harden so that it will bring the mixture together well.

You can use either a dehydrator or your oven to 'bake' the cookies. If using the oven, pre-heat it to 100°C and line an oven tray with baking paper.

Place cashew nuts, ginger, seeds, goji berries, vanilla and salt in a food processor and blend for 10 seconds to break down ingredients. Add coconut oil and honey, and blend further until well mixed and the texture is sticky.

Place 2 tablespoon-sized heaps in one hand, and roll each into a ball. Place onto dehydrator tray or oven tray and flatten carefully with your palm. Leave in dehydrator for 8 hours, or in oven for 30 minutes, until preferred consistency is reached.

"These delicious healthy cookies take me back to my childhood. The honey creates a soft, chewy texture, seeds add extra crunch, and the goji berries are little pops of sweetness. A great option for kids lunches."

RASPBERRY, ALMOND & YOGHURT MUFFINS

Recipe by **ELEANOR OZICH** *from Petite Kitchen*

MAKES: 10–12 STANDARD MUFFINS | PREP TIME: 15 MINS | COOK TIME: 20–25 MINS | SKILL LEVEL: 1 (EASY)

INGREDIENTS

¾ cup plain unsweetened yoghurt, or coconut cream

3 free-range eggs

½ cup (115 g) coconut oil, or unsalted butter, melted

¼ cup liquid honey

1 cup (145 g) buckwheat flour, or flour of your choice

1 cup (90 g) almond meal, or ground almonds

zest and juice of 1 lemon

1 tsp baking soda

1 tbsp apple cider vinegar

1 punnet fresh raspberries

GF

METHOD

Pre-heat the oven to 160°C. Grease the holes of a standard muffin tin, or line with paper cases.

Place the yoghurt or coconut cream, eggs and coconut oil or butter in a food processor. Blend to a smooth batter.

Add the honey, flour, almond meal or ground almonds, lemon zest and juice, baking soda and vinegar. Pulse until well combined. Divide the batter among the prepared muffin holes, and then top with the fresh raspberries.

Bake for 20–25 minutes, or until a skewer inserted into the centre of a muffin comes out clean. Cool on a wire rack.

TIP

These gorgeously moist muffins are naturally free of gluten, and are sweetened with a touch of honey. The addition of yoghurt gives a beautiful light and fluffy texture, although coconut cream works wonderfully also as a dairy-free alternative.

"My family and I often enjoy these on a sunny Saturday morning. A thick spread of butter is appropriate, although not entirely necessary!"

FRUITY BANANA, CARROT & PINEAPPLE CAKE

Recipe by **NIKI BEZZANT** *from Healthy Food Guide*

SERVES: 16 | PREP TIME: 20 MINS | COOK TIME: 45–50 MINS | SKILL LEVEL: 1 (EASY)

INGREDIENTS

1½ cups plain flour
½ cup coconut flour
2 tsp baking powder
1 tsp baking soda
1½ tsp ground cinnamon
½ cup pineapple pieces (see tip)
1 cup grated carrot (2 carrots)
3–4 ripe bananas, mashed (2 cups pulp)
2 eggs, beaten
¼ cup macadamia or vegetable oil
½ cup low-fat plain unsweetened yoghurt
¼ cup coconut threads

METHOD

Pre-heat oven to 190°C. Line a 20 cm round cake tin with baking paper.

Sift together flours, baking powder, baking soda and cinnamon. Stir in pineapple and carrot.

In a separate bowl, combine banana, eggs, oil and yoghurt. Add to the flour mixture and stir until the mixture is just combined. Spoon into the prepared tin. Sprinkle coconut over the top.

Bake for 30 minutes, then put tinfoil over the cake to prevent the coconut burning. Continue to bake for a further 15 minutes, or until a skewer inserted into the centre comes out clean. Remove from oven and allow to cool in the tin. Store in an airtight container and eat within two days.

TIP

If you want to make this more like a traditional carrot cake, you could go with a cream cheese icing instead of the coconut on top.

"Pineapple is one of my favourite fruits; its gorgeous natural sweetness means this pretty cake doesn't need any added sugar."

PASSIONFRUIT & MACADAMIA COCONUT TRUFFLES

Recipe by **MEGAN MAY** *from Little Bird*

MAKES: 12 | PREP TIME: 15 MINS | SKILL LEVEL: 1 (EASY)

INGREDIENTS

¾ cup (115 g) macadamia nuts

1 cup dried or desiccated coconut

4 tbsp local raw honey, coconut nectar or raw agave

zest of 1 lemon

pinch of sea salt

¼ tsp vanilla paste or seeds of 1 vanilla bean

1 tbsp freeze-dried passionfruit powder (I use Fresh-As brand)

extra dried or desiccated coconut, for rolling

DF GF

METHOD

Place ½ cup of the macadamias in a food processor and blend into a smooth butter (this is how you can make your own fresh macadamia butter).

Now add half the coconut, along with the honey (or sweetener of choice), lemon zest, salt and vanilla to the food processor, and blend together until well combined – the resulting mixture will be quite sticky.

At this point add remaining coconut and macadamias as well as passionfruit powder, and blend for 5–10 seconds until the mixture comes together but some texture remains. If the mixture is too sticky to work with (particularly if you have used honey), add small amounts of extra coconut until you can form a ball with it.

Take tablespoon amounts of the mixture and form each into a soft ball, then roll in extra coconut. Store in an airtight container in the fridge or freezer.

NOTE

Freeze-dried products have not been heated or had preservatives added to them. The water is removed from fresh produce at very low temperatures, which helps retain all the intense flavour and nutrients of the original produce.

"My childhood was filled with many a passionfruit. The sweet tanginess was a family favourite and we always had them growing in the garden. These truffles are absolutely delicious, and you know while you are treating yourself you're nurturing yourself, too."

DATE & CASHEW CARAMEL SLICE

Recipe by **NADIA LIM**

MAKES: 25 PIECES | PREP TIME: 30 MINS, PLUS CHILLING | COOK TIME: 15 MINS | SKILL LEVEL: 1 (EASY)

INGREDIENTS

Base

¾ cup rolled oats or ground almonds for gluten free

¾ cup long-thread desiccated coconut

1 tbsp good-quality dark cocoa powder

6 Medjool dates, pitted

½ cup raw almonds

pinch of salt

6–8 tbsp coconut oil, melted

Filling

3 cups dried pitted dates

¾ cup boiling water

2 cups cashew nuts, softened (see note)

¼ cup pure maple syrup

½ cup coconut oil, melted

1 tsp vanilla extract

Topping

150–200 g good-quality dark chocolate (60–72% cocoa solids)

1 tsp neutral-flavoured oil (e.g. walnut, canola, soy)

⅓ cup walnuts, chopped (optional)

1–2 tbsp long-thread desiccated coconut (optional)

GF

METHOD

For the base: pre-heat oven to 180°C. Lightly grease a 20 cm square baking tin and line the bottom and sides with baking paper.

Place oats/ground almonds, coconut, cocoa, dates, almonds and salt in a food processor and blitz until a fine, crumbly texture. Drizzle in coconut oil and pulse until well combined and the mixture holds together when you pinch it between your fingers.

Put mixture into the prepared tin, pressing down firmly with the back of a spoon or spatula. Bake for 10–15 minutes until light golden. Set aside in the fridge to cool while you make the caramel.

For the filling: place dates and water in a medium-sized pot and boil, stirring frequently, until dates are very soft and mushy and all the water has evaporated. Place dates in the food processor, along with softened cashew nuts, maple syrup, coconut oil and vanilla. Blitz until nice and smooth – this will take at least a few minutes. Scrape down the sides of the food processor a few times to make sure everything has been blended in.

Spread filling all over the base in the baking tin. Place in the fridge to set for at least 4 hours, or the freezer for at least 2 hours, until the filling is firm.

For the topping: melt chocolate in the top of a double boiler or in a glass bowl set above a small pot of simmering water. Mix in oil, then pour all over the filling and spread it over evenly. Scatter with walnuts and coconut, if using. Return to the fridge for about 20 minutes, or until set. If it still seems a bit soft, return to the fridge/freezer for a little longer.

To serve: cut into about 25 pieces using a long, sharp serrated knife. I find it easiest to flip the whole slice upside-down and cut through the base down. The slice will keep for up to a week in the fridge and also freezes well.

TIPS

To make softened cashew nuts, either soak in cold water overnight or boil cashew nuts in a pot of water for about 15 minutes until soft. Drain and use.

Use dairy-free chocolate if you want to make this receipt diary free as well.

"People are gobsmacked when I tell them there's no refined sugar, dairy or gluten in this delicious slice. Enjoy!"

LAURENT LOUDEAC

SAVOURY SNACKS

QUICHE LORRAINE

Recipe by **LAURENT LOUDEAC** *from Hippopotamus*

SERVINGS: 8 | PREP TIME: 20 MINS, PLUS CHILLING | COOK TIME: 30 MINS | SKILL LEVEL: 2 (MODERATE)

INGREDIENTS

Pastry

300 g plain flour

150 g cold unsalted butter, chopped

½ tsp salt

a little iced water

Filling

200 g lightly smoked speck, cut into lardons

½ onion, chopped

8 eggs

60 g crème fraîche

½ tsp salt

freshly ground black pepper, to taste

2 tbsp parsley, chopped

100 g grated Gruyère cheese (or tasty will do)

METHOD

To make the pastry, process flour, butter and salt in a food processor until mixture resembles crumbs. Add 2 tablespoons iced water and process again until the mixture just comes together, adding more water if necessary. Turn out onto a lightly floured work surface and shape into a ball. Enclose in plastic wrap and refrigerate for 30 minutes.

Pre-heat the oven to 190°C. Dust work surface with extra flour, and roll out pastry until 3 mm thick – big enough to line and slightly overlap a standard quiche tin, ensuring there are no holes or cracks. Using your fingers, press top edge of pastry to form a thick, flat edge, and refrigerate for 15 minutes.

Cover pastry with baking paper and fill with baking beans or rice. Bake for 10 minutes, then remove beans and paper and bake for a further 5 minutes or until base is dry. Put aside to cool.

Place speck and onion in a pan and fry gently until golden-brown, discarding excess fat by draining it off through a sieve. Whisk eggs and crème fraîche with salt in a bowl, until combined. Season with pepper and mix parsley in.

Place pre-baked tart shell on an oven tray. Scatter pastry base with speck and onion, then pour egg mixture over and sprinkle cheese on top. Bake for 15 minutes or until puffed and golden. Cool for 10 minutes, then serve with a green salad.

"Accompanied by a salad, this makes for a great light lunch (depending on how much cheese you put in it!)."

BACON & EGG PIE

Recipe by **RUTH PRETTY** *from Ruth Pretty Catering*

SERVINGS: 6–12 | PREP TIME: 45 MINS | COOK TIME: 45 MINS | SKILL LEVEL: 2 (MODERATE)

INGREDIENTS

Pie

250–300 g puff pastry

200 g rindless middle bacon rashers

10 eggs

1 tbsp onion, finely chopped

1 tbsp fresh parsley finely chopped

freshly ground black pepper

½ tsp flaky sea salt

Glaze

1 egg yolk

1 tbsp water

METHOD

Take a deep-sided, round 17 cm cake tin. Our tin has a depth of 4½ cm. On a lightly floured surface, roll out about a third of the pastry and use the tin base as a guide to cut out the base of the pie. Place this into the tin.

Roll out another third and cut out a second round the same size, to use as the top of the pie. Place on a lightly floured tray.

Roll out the remaining pastry to a strip which will form the sides of the pie. Make it the same height as your tin and long enough to go all the way around the inside. Join the pastry if you do not have the full length in one piece.

Place pastry strip inside the tin, around the sides. Using your fingertips, gently push the edge of the base onto the sides to adhere and form a seal. Place the tin and tray in the refrigerator to rest pastry for 20 minutes. Pre-heat the oven to 210°C.

Cut each bacon rasher into three. Line pastry base with half the bacon, allowing the bacon slices to sit side by side rather than overlapping. Break whole eggs into a cup, one by one, and gradually place each one onto bacon, taking care that the yolks remain whole. Sprinkle onion, parsley, pepper and salt onto eggs. Lay bacon over remaining eggs.

Make a very small hole in the centre of the pastry lid. (A piping nozzle is ideal to do this.) Brush a very small border around the inside edge of the lid with cold water. Place lid on pie. Gently fork around lid edge to seal the pie and, if you wish, use any leftover pastry to make a decorative twist to go around the pie.

Place egg yolk and water in a bowl. Mix together and brush the glaze onto the lid. Place the pie into the oven. After 20 minutes, reduce the heat to 180°C. Cook for a further 25 minutes, or until the pie is light golden-brown and the base is cooked through.

Cool and serve, or place in refrigerator to serve within two days. When the pie is cold, tip out of the tin and invert onto a serving plate.

TIPS

If you can, use streaky bacon as it has the best flavour and it is malleable. Aim to use free range eggs as they taste better and have better colour. By the way, not all pastry and especially puff pastry at the supermarket, is created equal. You definitely need one made with butter.

SPANAKOPITA

Recipe by the team at **DIMITRIS GREEK FOOD**

MAKES: ABOUT 20 | PREP TIME: 20 MINS | COOK TIME: 20–25 MINS | SKILL LEVEL: 1 (EASY)

INGREDIENTS

3–4 bunches spinach, depending on size
1 medium-sized onion
1 stick celery
400 g good-quality Greek feta
2 medium-sized eggs
1 tbsp olive oil
1 packet filo pastry
vegetable oil, to oil the pastry

METHOD

Pre-heat oven to 180°C fan-bake.

Wash and dry spinach, onion and celery. Dice onion and celery and gently fry in butter or oil in a medium-sized frying pan until soft. Cool.

Cut spinach into strips about 2 cm wide and place in a large bowl. Add onion and celery. Crumble feta into the bowl.

Break eggs into the bowl. Add olive oil, and season with salt and pepper to taste. Mix ingredients by hand until thoroughly combined.

Lay filo pastry out on a clean bench with one of the short sides facing you. Cut filo into three equal columns (cut top to bottom). Place about a tablespoon of spinach mixture at one end. Take a bottom corner of the top two sheets of filo and fold them over diagonally to make a triangle, with the bottom edge of the filo lined up with the long side. Flip triangle vertically, with the bottom corner ending up at the top of the triangle, enclosing the first fold of filo. Flip the triangle diagonally again, then vertically again to enclose the filling fully. Repeat until all filo pastry is used.

Place triangle on a lined baking tray. Repeat with remaining filling and filo. Once tray is filled with triangles, brush oil on top. Bake for about 20–30 minutes or until golden-brown on top. Leave to cool on the tray for a few minutes, then transfer to a wire rack to finish cooling. Serve and enjoy.

BUCKWHEAT BUTTERMILK BLINIS

Recipe by **SUE FLEISCHL** *from The Great Catering Company*

MAKES: ABOUT 40 | PREP TIME: 15 MINS, PLUS RESTING | COOK TIME: 25 MINS | SKILL LEVEL: 1 (EASY)

INGREDIENTS

2¼ tsp active dried yeast
½ cup warm water
pinch of sugar
1 tbsp (15 g) salted butter, melted (plus extra for cooking)
½ cup buttermilk
½ tsp sugar
2 eggs, separated
½ cup all-purpose flour
½ cup buckwheat flour
pinch of salt

METHOD

Mix yeast, water and sugar in a large bowl and leave for 30 minutes until frothy.

In a separate bowl, mix butter, buttermilk, sugar and egg yolks together and add to yeast mixture.

In another bowl, combine flours and salt, and add to the wet mixture.

Beat egg whites to soft peaks and fold into blini mixture.

Heat a large frying pan over a low-to-medium heat. Add dessertspoons of blini batter and cook for 1–2 minutes, or until golden. Flip and cook the other side. They can be made a day ahead and reheated or wrapped and frozen.

Serve with any of the following toppings: medium-boiled egg mashed with a little mayo and chives; sour cream and salmon caviar; crème fraîche and smoked salmon; crayfish with chopped mango and avocado; cooked turkey and cranberry sauce; pulled pork and coleslaw.

INDIAN-SPICED CORN FRITTERS

Recipe by **SIMON GAULT**

SERVINGS: 4–6 | PREP TIME: 10 MINS | COOK TIME: 20–25 MINS | SKILL LEVEL: 1 (EASY)

INGREDIENTS

- 160 g (1 large) onion, chopped finely
- a little oil, for cooking
- 100 g mascarpone
- 4 tbsp Simon Gault Home Cuisine Indian Seasoning
- 20 ml lemon juice
- 2 cups plain flour
- 2 tsp salt
- 2 tsp baking powder
- ½ tsp freshly ground black pepper
- 4 eggs
- ½ cup milk
- 250 g Parmesan, grated
- 600 g corn kernels
- 100 ml soda water
- 50 ml extra virgin olive oil
- fresh pea tendrils, to garnish (optional)

METHOD

Gently pan-fry onion in a little oil until softened. Set aside to cool.

In a small bowl, mix mascarpone, 2 tablespoons of Indian seasoning and lemon juice together and set aside until required.

Put flour, salt, baking powder and black pepper in a bowl and mix together. Add eggs and milk to create a thick batter, then add onion, Parmesan, corn, remaining Indian seasoning and soda water. Mix this through the batter.

In a non-stick frying pan, heat olive oil until hot and add a generous spoonful of batter mixture for each fritter. Cook until golden-brown on both sides and firm to the touch, about 4–5 minutes. Repeat until all the batter is cooked.

To serve, place the fritters on a board with a heaped tablespoon of the Indian-spiced mascarpone, and garnish.

SAVOURY BRIOCHE

Recipe by **KIM EVANS** *from Little & Friday*

MAKES: 9 | PREP TIME: 20 MINS, PLUS DOUGH | COOK TIME: 20 MINS | SKILL LEVEL: 2 (MODERATE)

INGREDIENTS

1 recipe brioche dough (see p.18)
½ cup basil pesto
1 cup crumbled feta
1 cup grated vintage tasty cheese
12 sun-dried tomatoes, chopped
2 cups fresh baby spinach
1 egg
2 tbsp milk

METHOD

Make brioche dough. Pre-heat oven to 180°C. Grease 9 Texas muffin tins or small tin cans.

On a floured bench, roll dough into a rectangle measuring approximately 45 cm x 20 cm and 1 cm thick. Position dough on the bench so the longer side is facing you.

Spread pesto over dough, ensuring it is fully covered. Scatter with feta and tasty cheese, and sprinkle with sun-dried tomatoes. Lastly, place a thick layer of spinach over the top. Starting on the longer side close to you, roll dough up away from you to form a long log. Using a sharp knife, slice into –pieces 5 cm thick – you should end up with nine scrolls. Place each scroll in a muffin tin. Beat egg and milk together and brush over tops of scrolls.

Bake for 20 minutes, or until golden brown. Allow to cool before removing from tins.

JANE
1850
1950

FRITTATA WITH ZUCCHINI & BASIL

Recipe by **MARTIN BOSLEY**

SERVINGS: 4 | PREP TIME: 20–25 MINS | SKILL LEVEL: 1 (EASY)

INGREDIENTS

1 small onion
2 cloves garlic
1 tbsp unsalted butter
200 g zucchini (2–4 depending on size)
6 large basil leaves
6 eggs
120 g grated Parmesan

GF

METHOD

Pre-heat oven to 180°C.

Peel and thinly slice onion, and peel and chop garlic. Melt butter in a shallow, oven-proof frying pan and cook onions and garlic until they have softened. Grate zucchini, stir into onion mixture and cook gently for 4 minutes.

Finely slice basil, add to the pan and remove from the heat, while you beat eggs and Parmesan together in a mixing bowl with a fork. Tip the contents of the bowl into the frying pan, fold everything together and return it to the stove. Cook over a low heat for a few minutes until a crust has formed on the bottom. Remove the pan from the heat, slide it into the oven and cook until the top is lightly coloured.

Remove from the oven and use a fish slice to lift the frittata from the pan. Cut into wedges and serve with a lightly dressed salad.

LAVOSH CRACKERS

Recipe by **MICHEL LOUWS** *from M&M Food & Drink*

SERVES: 6–8 | PREP TIME: 15 MINS | COOK TIME: 15 MINS | SKILL LEVEL: 2 (MODERATE)

INGREDIENTS

2 cups plain flour
1 tsp baking powder
½ tsp salt, plus extra for topping
⅔ cups warm water
⅔ cup canola oil
1 egg white, whisked
2 tbsp black sesame seeds
2 tbsp white sesame seeds

DF

METHOD

Pre-heat oven to 160–180°C.

Sift flour, baking powder and salt into a bowl, add water and oil and mix until combined. The mixture should be easily spreadable; if too stiff, add a little extra water.

Use an offset spatula to spread thinly on non-stick baking mat or baking paper. Brush gently with egg white, then top with extra salt and sesame seeds. You can go crazy with the seasonings – from Japanese rice seasonings to home-made concoctions using chilli, cumin seeds, poppy seeds (toasted, of course) or baharat spice, or plain cracked pepper and sea salt – or how about mustard and fennel with cured kahawai?

Oh yeah... don't forget to bake them – depending on your oven, it will take about 15 minutes till they're golden.

CHICKEN, LEEK & MUSHROOM PIE

Recipe by **TONY ASTLE** *from Antoine's*

SERVINGS: 6 | PREP TIME: 45 MINS, PLUS OVERNIGHT | COOK TIME: 1 HOUR | SKILL LEVEL: 2 (MODERATE)

INGREDIENTS

Leek and mushroom mix
2 large onions
4 large leeks
100 g butter
125 g shiitake mushroom caps
150 g oyster (phoenix tail) mushrooms
150 g Swiss brown mushrooms
250 ml Madeira or medium sherry
750 ml cream
2 tbsp fresh tarragon or sage, chopped
3 cloves garlic, chopped

Chicken filling
1 large free-range chicken
2 large onions
4 whole cloves
3 large carrots
4 bay leaves
½ tbsp salt
6 peppercorns
250 ml fresh, well-flavoured chicken stock

To assemble
butter and flour, for pie dish
about 200 g puff pastry
beaten egg, to wash

METHOD

Finely chop onions and leeks (not too much of the green part). Melt butter in a large saucepan or heavy-based pot. Add onion and leek to the pan and slowly sweat, not allowing them to brown (approximately 2 minutes). Slice and add all the mushrooms and cook for a further 5 minutes, stirring frequently.

Add Madeira or sherry, then cream. Stir well, then add herbs and garlic. Bring to a simmer and cook for approximately 25 minutes over a low heat, being careful not to let the mixture catch on the bottom of the pan. When the mixture has reduced by about a quarter, add salt and freshly ground black or white pepper to taste. Remove from the heat and allow to cool to room temperature before refrigerating. This mixture is best made the day before it is required.

To make the filling, place chicken in a large pot. Stud onions with cloves and roughly slice carrots, then add to chicken, together with bay leaves, salt and peppercorns. Cover the chicken completely with water. Bring to a boil over a high heat, then turn down and simmer for 25 minutes.

Remove chicken from heat, cover and cool in the cooking liquid. When at room temperature, remove chicken from pot and place in a non-corrosive container. Add stock, making sure to cover completely. Refrigerate until required.

To assemble the pie, grease a pie dish well with butter and dust with flour. Divide pastry in two, one piece smaller than the other (for the lid), and roll out to approximately 3 mm thick. Line pie dish, letting some of the pastry overlap the rim. Refrigerate until required.

Pre-heat the oven to 180°C. Remove chicken from stock and discard skin. Remove chicken meat from bones and cut into large chunks. Mix with the cold mushroom mixture. Place into the pie crust, heaped to the top. Apply pastry lid, bringing the overlap over to seal the pie. Wash top of pie with beaten egg and bake for 1 hour, until cooked.

TIPS

Make sure you use good-quality butter puff pastry. If you have time to make your own, the rough puff pastry recipe in the *Edmonds Cookery Book* is fantastic. If making pastry, make sure the butter is cold from the fridge and be sure to be as quick as possible when making.

When cooking chicken, do not overcook. Follow the recipe! Definitely make the pie mixture the day before; it's best cold from the fridge when making the pie.

Serve with a fresh green salad, tossed with buffalo mozzarella.

LAMB SAUSAGE ROLLS WITH MINTED PEA PURÉE

Recipe by **KATE FAY** *from Cibo*

SERVINGS: 4 | PREP TIME: 50 MINS | COOK TIME: 3 1/4 HOURS, PLUS OVERNIGHT | SKILL LEVEL: 2 (MODERATE)

INGREDIENTS

Sausage rolls

olive oil, for frying

500 g cooked lamb shank meat (approx. 1.2kg uncooked)

2 tbsp butter

1 medium-sized onion, roughly chopped

½ head garlic, cloves separated

1 small carrot, roughly chopped

1 stick of celery, roughly chopped

½ leek, roughly chopped

2 sprigs fresh thyme

1 sprig fresh rosemary

about 2 cups (500 ml) beef stock

12 sheets of filo pastry

melted butter, for brushing

Pea purée

2 cups (260 g) frozen baby peas

50 g butter

¼ small brown onion, finely diced

2 cloves garlic, crushed

¼ cup cream

fresh mint leaves

3 tbsp olive oil

Mint jelly

225 g sugar

½ cup white wine

½ cup water

3 cups fresh mint leaves

½ onion, sliced

5 cloves garlic

agar for setting

METHOD

Pre-heat the oven to 170°C and prepare vegetables. Heat a frying pan to moderate heat and add olive oil, then sear lamb all over, until caramelised a deep golden brown. Remove from pan and place in a casserole dish. Add butter to the pan, then onion, garlic and vegetables and cook until coloured and caramelised. Add this mixture to the lamb, add herbs, and season well with salt and black pepper. Cover with beef stock, then cover with a lid or tinfoil and place in the oven for 3 hours until lamb is tender. Cool. Remove lamb from the liquid and shred the meat. Strain the stock, and process 1 cup of the braised vegetables in a blender, then mix these with the meat. Season the mix again, and add extra herbs to taste. Roll into a sausage shape (70 cm long, 3.5 cm high and 2 cm deep) and chill in the fridge overnight.

Next day, pre-heat the oven to 170°C. Divide meat sausage into 12. Brush a sheet of filo with melted butter and fold it in half lengthways. Brush again with butter. Fold in half again and brush with butter once more. Fold into a strip a third of the length. Place a cylinder of meat at one end and roll the strip up, sealing the end with butter. Repeat. Place rolls on a baking sheet lined with baking paper, bake for 15 minutes, until golden brown.

For the pea purée, cook peas in boiling water for 2–3 minutes, until tender. Drain. Melt butter in a frying pan over medium heat. Add onion and garlic and cook for 2–3 minutes until softened. Add peas, then cream, and bring to the boil. Stir for 1 minute or until heated through. Remove from the heat and add mint leaves. Process until smooth, then add olive oil and season to taste with salt and pepper. Pass the mix through a fine sieve and serve on sausage rolls.

For the mint jelly, bring all ingredients except agar to the boil and simmer for about 10 minutes, then set aside to cool and infuse for 2 hours. Strain, and measure the liquid. Add 2 grams agar for every 100 ml of liquid and bring back up to the boil. Simmer for 5–8 minutes, until all the agar is incorporated. Strain again and place in the fridge to set. To serve, blend until smooth and place in a squeeze bottle.

You may wish to add a pea salad of cooked peas, fresh pea leaves and tendrils and blanched sugarsnap peas, tossed with olive oil and shredded fresh mint.

"I've taken the lamb sausage from finger food to the plate; a nod to the past while celebrating the future."

SAVOURY CRÊPES

Recipe by **JACOB BROWN** *from The Larder*

MAKES: 8 | PREP TIME: 5 MINS, PLUS RESTING | COOK TIME: 30 MINS | SKILL LEVEL: 1 (EASY)

INGREDIENTS

60 g plain flour
pinch of salt
50 g caster sugar
60 ml cream
1 egg
160 ml milk
15 ml butter, melted
oil, for cooking

METHOD

Combine flour, salt and sugar in a bowl. In a separate bowl, beat together cream, egg and milk. Add this to the flour mixture, stirring with the whisk to combine. Leave the crêpe mix to sit for 1 hour, then add melted butter.

Heat a non-stick pan over medium heat. Lightly season pan with oil, then ladle in just enough batter to thinly coat the pan, tilting it to produce a uniformly thin crêpe. Cook over a moderate heat until bubbles appear on the surface. Gently flip the crêpe over and cook the other side until a pale golden colour. Remove from the pan and repeat the process until all the crêpe batter has been used.

TIP

Crêpes are delicious served with Gruyère and shavings of ham from the leg, or if you want something sweet try citrus yoghurt and fresh berries.

LEEK & CHEESE TARTS

Recipe by **SUE FLEISCHL** *from The Great Catering Company*

MAKES: 30 | PREP TIME: 40 MINS, PLUS RESTING/COOLING | COOK TIME: 15 MINS | SKILL LEVEL: 2 (MODERATE)

INGREDIENTS

Pastry

400 g plain flour

large pinch of sweet paprika powder

pinch of salt

200 g salted butter, chilled and cut into cubes

110 ml chilled water

Filling

1 leek, sliced finely

1 tbsp butter

150 g feta (your favourite variety), crumbled

150 g bocconcini, cut into little pieces

100 g grated Parmesan

½ tsp freshly ground black pepper

To finish

1 egg, beaten

1 tsp cumin seeds

METHOD

For the pastry: place flour, paprika, salt and butter in a food processor and pulse until a crumb consistency. Add chilled water and pulse to just combine. Turn out onto a floured bench and lightly knead to just combine. Flatten slightly (this makes it easier to roll later), enclose in plastic wrap and leave in the fridge to rest for at least 1 hour.

Place rested pastry on a lightly floured bench and roll out evenly to ½ cm thick. Cut out 10 cm circles (or any size you like).

For the filling: slowly cook leek in butter until soft. Cool, then mix with feta, bocconcini, Parmesan and pepper.

To finish: pre-heat oven to 200°C. Place dessertspoons of filling in the middle of each pastry circle, leaving a 2 cm edge. Pinch the edges of the pastry up around the sides of the filling, pressing firmly to prevent them popping open during baking. The tarts should be approximately 2 cm high and 6 cm in diameter. Place tarts on greased or lined baking trays, spaced slightly apart.

Brush the top edges of the pastry with beaten egg and sprinkle the filling with 3–6 cumin seeds, to taste. Rest for 30 minutes in the fridge, then bake for about 15 minutes until golden brown.

TIPS

The pastry can be made two days ahead, and stored well wrapped in the fridge. The tarts can be cooked a day ahead and reheated when ready to serve. You can vary the fillings also – try spinach or kale and blue cheese.

"Leek and cheese is a winning combination, and with a generous amount of cheese, these become a mouthful of gooey yumminess."

MICHELLE'S KRANSKY ROLLS

Recipe by **MICHELLE PATTISON**

MAKES: 12 | PREP TIME: 10 MINS | COOK TIME: 15–18 MINS | SKILL LEVEL: 1 (EASY)

INGREDIENTS

1 sheet butter puff pastry (24 cm x 24 cm)

egg wash: 1 egg whisked together with 1 tsp water

12 Kransky sausages (I use Verkerk's)

¼ cup poppy seeds (or you can use black and white sesame seeds)

METHOD

Pre-heat the oven to 200°C fan-bake (or 220°C regular). Grease an oven tray.

Place pastry sheet on a wooden board. Brush top of the pastry with egg wash. Cut into 12 even strips (2 cm x 24 cm per strip).

Prick each Kransky several times with a fork. Starting at one end of the Kransky, wrap pastry strip in a spiral down to the other end, egg-wash-side down. Trim ends if necessary and press against a loop of pastry underneath the Kransky, pressing firmly to seal. Place roll (sealed side down) on the oven tray.

Brush top side of pastry with egg wash and sprinkle with a small amount of poppy seeds. Repeat with remaining Kranskies.

Put Kransky rolls into the oven and bake for 15 minutes, or until the pastry is cooked and golden. These can be served hot or cold but either way, make sure there's plenty of tomato sauce!

"These rolls are always a hit at kids parties; they're for the young – and the young at heart!"

BAOS (CHINESE STEAMED PORK BUNS)

Recipe by **ANTHONY HOY FONG**

MAKES: 30–40 | PREP TIME: 5½ HOURS | SKILL LEVEL: 2 (MODERATE)

INGREDIENTS

Pork filling

1 kg boneless pork shoulder, cubed

4 cloves garlic, peeled and minced

2 cm piece ginger, peeled and minced

3 tbsp hoisin sauce

¼ cup soy sauce

2 tsp sugar

1½ tsp salt

¼ tsp ground black pepper

2 tbsp canola oil

3 tbsp cornflour

2 tbsp water

Dough

400 ml milk, warmed

3 tbsp sugar

5 tsp active dry yeast

1,150 g high-grade flour, plus extra for kneading

220 g cornflour

1½ tsp salt

¼ cup (35 g) pork fat or lard (you can skim and reserve clean pork fat from when you cook pork)

up to 200 ml warm water, as needed

METHOD

Filling: this can be done a day ahead of making buns, or while dough is resting. Trim pork of any tough sinew (but leave the fat on). Make a marinade by combining garlic, ginger, hoisin sauce, soy sauce, sugar, salt and black pepper together. Pour marinade over pork in a large bowl. Mix, cover and marinate for 30 minutes.

Set a large, heavy pot over a high heat and add oil. Once hot, add drained pork pieces (lift them out with a slotted spoon) and brown well all over, about 5–6 minutes. Add marinade, then enough water to just cover pork. Bring to the boil, reduce heat and simmer for 1 hour, uncovered, until pork is very tender and liquid has reduced by two-thirds.

Remove pork from pot and allow to cool slightly before dicing finely into 1 cm pieces. Mix cornflour and water together, then pour into sauce and stir until thickened. Fold diced pork back into thickened braising liquid. Remove from heat, allow to cool, then refrigerate until completely cold.

Dough: in a large mixing bowl combine milk, sugar and yeast. Set aside for 15 minutes to allow yeast to activate – it will form bubbles and become slightly frothy when ready. Sift flour, cornflour and salt together into a separate bowl. Cut pork fat into dry ingredients until there are only small pieces of it through the dry mixture.

Combine dry mixture with milk/yeast liquid and half the water. Mix with your hands until it forms a single mass of dough. Add remaining water only as required, until the dough is workable and smooth (but not too sticky). If it gets too sticky, add a bit more flour. Once dough is kneaded and smooth, return to bowl and cover with a damp cloth. Place in a warm, dry spot (hot-water cupboard or oven warmer drawer on low work well) and let it rest for 2–3 hours or until tripled in volume. In the meantime, take some baking or greaseproof paper and cut out about 30 square pieces (10cm x 10 cm).

Once risen, tip dough out onto a floured surface and knead for 15–20 minutes until completely smooth. This ensures you don't get too many large air bubbles in the finished dough. Once smooth, return dough to mixing bowl and place a towel over the top (so it doesn't dry out as you set up to prepare the buns).

Assembly: Working with 2–3 pieces at a time, form dough into golf-ball-sized pieces. Flatten out to about ¾-cm-thick 'pancakes' in the centre of your palm. Press lightly in the centre to make a small dimple. Place a heaped tablespoon of filling in the dimple, then fold in the edges and pinch together tightly to seal. Place ball, seam-side down, in the centre of a paper square. Set on a baking tray while the rest of the buns are prepared. Place tray back in a warm spot, covered with a towel, to rise again for 1 hour.

Steaming: Set up your steamer (a multi-layered steamer works well). Fill the bottom of the steamer with 2–3 cm of water. Tie a teatowel around the lid to catch any condensation drips that would otherwise drip onto the buns. Place buns in steamer baskets, leaving 1–2 cm of space between the paper squares so there's room for buns to expand. Steam buns on a rapid boil for 15–17 minutes until the bread is light, fluffy and shiny on the surface. Serve hot with a little extra soy sauce on the side.

MUSSEL FRITTERS

Recipe by **SIMON GAULT**

SERVINGS: 4–6 | PREP TIME: 30 MINS | COOK TIME: 20 MINS | SKILL LEVEL: 2 (MODERATE)

INGREDIENTS

600 g mussel meat (about 3½ kg fresh mussels)
100 ml white wine
100 g mascarpone
zest of 1 lemon
20 ml lemon juice
250 g Parmesan cheese
160 g finely chopped onion
2 cups flour
2 tsp salt
2 tsp baking powder
½ tsp freshly ground
black pepper
4 eggs
1 cup milk
50 ml extra virgin olive oil
2 tbsp capers
100 ml canola oil
fresh pea tendrils to garnish

METHOD

Clean mussels thoroughly and place them in a saucepan with wine. Cover and bring to a simmer. With a spoon, rotate mussels in the wine. As the shells open, remove them from the saucepan and allow to cool. Discard any mussels that don't open. To de-beard your mussels, pull the threads down towards the pointy end of the shell, discarding the brown foot and any muscle attached to the shell.

Remove mussel meat from the shells, then remove tongues and the main (round) muscle. Cut mussels into halves or thirds depending on size.

In a small bowl, mix mascarpone, lemon zest and juice together and set aside until required. Grate Parmesan and chop onion.

Put flour, salt, baking powder and pepper in a bowl and mix together. Add eggs and milk to create a thick batter, and then add Parmesan, onion and mussel meat. Mix through the batter.

In a non-stick pan, heat a splash of olive oil until hot and add a generous spoonful of batter for each fritter. Cook until golden brown on both sides and firm to the touch. Repeat until all the batter is cooked. Keep warm or reheat in a microwave before serving.

If capers are salted, soak in water for about 10 minutes. Heat canola oil until it shimmers and fry capers until crispy. Remove and drain on paper towels. Place fritters on a board draped with baking paper, and serve with a heaped tablespoonful of mascarpone and sprinkled with fried capers. Garnish with pea tendrils.

"I have early memories of my Dad going snorkeling around the wharf and rocks at Paihia, looking for mussels. By adding a touch of cheese, removing all those tough bits, and not overcooking the mussels, you end up with a fritter that says 'New Zealand', says 'unique' and says 'damned good'."

MINCE & CHEESE PIES

Recipe by **SARAH & MARTIN ASPINWALL** *from Canterbury Cheesemongers*

SERVINGS: 4 | PREP TIME: 90 MINS, INCLUDING COOKING | COOK TIME: 30 MINS | SKILL LEVEL: 2 (MODERATE)

INGREDIENTS

Filling base

½ small onion

1 small carrot

½ small stick of celery

2 tsp olive oil

200 g good-quality beef mince

200 g skirt or chuck steak, chopped

Seasonings

1 bay leaf

½ tsp smoked ground paprika

1 tsp chopped fresh thyme

zest of 1 lemon

2 cloves garlic, crushed and chopped

salt and pepper to taste

Sauce

2 grated tomatoes (skins discarded)

2 tsp tomato purée

2 tsp Worcestershire sauce

Pies

600 g rough puff flaky pastry, chilled

80 g mature Cheddar, grated

80 g vintage Gouda, grated

80 g Taleggio, cut into 4 slices

METHOD

Finely chop onion, carrot and celery. Heat oil in a medium-sized saucepan and fry vegetables until soft (4–5 minutes). Add meats and cook until brown and any moisture has evaporated. Add seasonings and cook for a further 2–3 minutes.

Next, add sauce ingredients and simmer gently with the lid on for 15 minutes, then take the lid off and cook for a further 15 minutes until the filling is fairly dry. Allow this to cool for 30 minutes.

Divide your pastry into four, then divide each one of these into a large half and a small half. Sprinkle a little flour on your work surface and roll out the larger pieces into rectangles, approximately 15 cm x 12 cm x 4 mm thick. Use these to line oval pie tins (size 13 cm x 10 cm x 3 cm deep). Roll out the tops to approximately 15 cm x 10 cm.

Pre-heat the oven to 180–190°C. Place 20 grams (a good pinch) of Cheddar cheese in the bottom of each pastry case, followed by a quarter of the filling. Top each with 20 grams of Gouda and a slice of Taleggio. Mix egg and milk to make egg wash. Brush pastry rims with egg wash and cover with the tops. Crimp the edges to seal them and use a knife to trim off excess pastry. Pierce through the top to make a steam hole, brush with egg wash and chill for 15 minutes.

Bake for 30 minutes.

TIPS

For our mince and cheese pies we use quality meat from our local butcher and proper cheese. The cheese is key; you need a good, flavourful mix and a generous amount. Our pies contain Barry's Bay Cheddar, Meyer Gouda and Taleggio from Italy – glorious!

CHEESE STRAWS

Recipe by **DAVID GRIFFITHS** *from Mister D*

MAKES: 24 | PREP TIME: 10 MINS, PLUS CHILLING | COOK TIME: 10–12 MINS | SKILL LEVEL: 1 (EASY)

INGREDIENTS

100 g plain flour
¼ tsp salt
½ tsp Espelette pepper (or a pinch of cayenne pepper), plus a little extra for topping
90 g butter
90 g grated Parmesan, plus a little extra for topping
1 egg, whisked
2 tsp sesame seeds (optional)
2 tsp breadcrumbs (optional)

METHOD

Place flour, salt, pepper and butter in a food processor and pulse until it is the texture of fine breadcrumbs. Place on the bench with the Parmesan and mix by hand to form a smooth dough. Do not knead or overwork; just bring it together with the warmth of your hands. Enclose in plastic food wrap and place in fridge to chill for 30 minutes.

Pre-heat the oven to 175°C.

Roll dough between two sheets of plastic food wrap to desired thickness, about 2 mm, and cut into rectangle shapes about 12 mm x 70 mm each. Brush with whisked egg and sprinkle with a little extra Parmesan and sesame seeds, breadcrumbs or pepper. Transfer to a baking tray and place in oven for 12–15 minutes until golden and crisp.

TIP

An easy way of grating the Parmesan is just to remove the rind, cut into cubes and whizz in a food processor until it reaches a crumb consistency.

OAT BISCUITS

Recipe by **JACOB BROWN** *from The Larder*

MAKES: 16 | PREP TIME: 10 MINS, PLUS CHILLING | COOK TIME: 12–15 MINS | SKILL LEVEL: 1 (EASY)

INGREDIENTS

1 cup (90 g) rolled oats
½ cup (80 g) wholemeal flour
⅓ cup (50 g) plain flour
2 tbsp grated Parmesan
1 tsp caster sugar
¼ tsp bicarbonate of soda
½ tsp salt
90 g butter, diced
2 egg whites
cheese, to serve

METHOD

Line two baking trays with baking paper.

In a food processor, process oats until a fine crumb. Add wholemeal and plain flours, Parmesan, sugar, bicarbonate of soda and salt.

With motor running, add butter. Process until mixture resembles breadcrumbs. With motor still running, add egg whites. Combine until mixture forms a ball.

Divide mixture in half. Roll out each half between floured baking paper into 23 cm circles. Place on prepared trays. Chill for 30 minutes.

Pre-heat oven to 200°C (180°C fan-bake).

Cut each dough circle into eight wedges. Bake for 12–15 minutes. Cool on a wire rack.

Serve biscuits with cheese.

WESTLAND-STYLE WHITEBAIT FRITTERS

Recipe by **THE KERR FAMILY** *from the Curly Tree Whitebait Company*

MAKES: 2–4 | PREP TIME: 5 MINS | COOK TIME: 4 MINS | SKILL LEVEL: 1 (EASY)

INGREDIENTS

500 g South Westland whitebait, fresh or frozen

1 large or 2 small eggs

rice bran oil spray, or a couple of knobs of butter

white bread, to serve

juice of 1 lemon

mint sauce

METHOD

If using frozen whitebait, let it thaw overnight in the fridge, then drain. Fresh whitebait – only in season, remember! – is best, of course.

Beat or whisk egg in a medium-to-large bowl. Mix lightly with whitebait and season with salt and pepper to taste (you could also use smoked garlic salt as an option).

Heat a hotplate or frying pan to medium-to-hot heat. Spray with oil or add butter.

Scoop whitebait mixture onto oil/butter, to whatever size you wish. Cook until golden underneath, then flip over and cook the other side.

Serve while still hot – traditionally on white bread, spread with a fat layer of butter, with lemon juice and mint sauce (an essential item in the West Coast cupboard!) on top. Fold in half and get stuck in.

"My Grandma Dulcie used to say 'the only thing you put into a good whitebait patty is more whitebait!'. At our place, we reckon all you need is a good piece of bread and butter, a drop of mint sauce or a squeeze of lemon, then let Dulcie's advice take care of the rest."

SPAGHETTI & CHEESE TOASTS

Recipe by **PETER GORDON**

SERVINGS: 6 | PREP TIME: 10 MINS | COOK TIME: 20 MINS | SKILL LEVEL: 1 (EASY)

INGREDIENTS

60 g butter, melted
6 slices soft white sandwich bread
1 x 400 g tin spaghetti in tomato sauce
3 tbsp grated Cheddar

METHOD

Pre-heat the oven to 180°C. Butter the bases of a six-hole patty pan or muffin tin.

Butter bread on one side, flip it over and press into the tin, butter-side down. Brush with remaining butter, making sure you use it all up. Spoon in spaghetti and top with cheese.

Bake until bread is crisp and golden, around 20 minutes. Leave in the tin for a few minutes to firm up, before gently removing. These are lovely eaten straight from the oven, or at room temperature.

TIP

You could make these in smaller tins and get even more!

"These spaghetti toasts couldn't be simpler – or tastier – if you tried. Buy just four ingredients and you'll be in blissful, tasty nirvana."

PASTIES

Recipe by **SUE FLEISCHL** *from The Great Catering Company*

MAKES: 4 | PREP TIME: 45 MINS, PLUS RESTING | COOK TIME: 55 MINS | SKILL LEVEL: 2 (MODERATE)

INGREDIENTS

Pastry

125 g butter, chilled and diced
125 g lard, chilled and diced
500 g plain flour
pinch of salt
6 tbsp chilled water
1 egg, beaten
2 tsp sesame seeds (optional)

Filling

1 onion, chopped finely
1 clove garlic, crushed
1 tsp olive oil
1 tsp butter
500 g skirt or scotch steak, trimmed and chopped into ½ cm cubes
1 medium-sized potato, peeled and chopped into ½ cm cubes
200 g swede, peeled and chopped into ½ cm cubes
2 tbsp chopped fresh thyme leaves
1 tbsp sea salt
2 tsp freshly ground black pepper

METHOD

Pre-heat oven to 200°C. Place butter, lard, flour and salt in a food processor. Pulse until crumbs form, then add water and pulse again to make a firm dough. Cut into four pieces, flatten slightly, wrap well and chill for at least 30 minutes.

For the filling: sauté onion and garlic together, gently, in olive oil and butter for 5 minutes, until soft. Mix with steak, potato, swede, thyme and salt and pepper. Set aside to cool.

Roll each pastry ball to ½ cm thick on a lightly floured surface, and cut each into a 23 cm round (we use a plate to do this). Firmly pack a quarter of the filling along the centre-line of each round. Brush all around the edge of the pastry with beaten egg, then bring the sides up around the filling and crimp together firmly.

Place on a lined or non-stick baking tray and brush with remaining beaten egg. Sprinkle with sesame seeds, if using, and chill for 30 minutes.

Bake pasties for 10 minutes, then lower the temperature to 180°C and bake for another 45 minutes.

BEN BAYLY

SWEET TREATS

CHOCOLATE-DIPPED HOKEY POKEY

Recipe by **BEN BAYLY**

SERVES/MAKES: 1 SLAB | PREP TIME: 30 MINS, PLUS SETTING | SKILL LEVEL: 2 (MODERATE)

INGREDIENTS

730 g sugar
340 g glucose powder
300 ml water
60 g baking soda (sodium bicarbonate)
300 g dark chocolate

GF

METHOD

Line a large baking tray with baking paper and grease it. I use a 20 cm x 30 cm tray.

Place sugar, glucose and water in a large saucepan, larger than you think you'll need. Place on the stove on a medium heat and bring to the boil to dissolve the sugar into a syrup. Now, you are going to cook the sugar syrup until the temperature is 155°C – at this stage the sugar is almost a caramel; it will just be beginning to colour and you will start to smell caramel flavours. This will take a good 10–15 minutes on the boil, depending on the size of your pot.

Remove from the heat and quickly whisk in the baking soda – but be careful! It's super-hot at this stage! The baking soda will make the hot sugar foam up – that's why you use an oversized saucepan. Don't over-mix, as you could knock out all the air bubbles.

Quickly pour the mix into the greased baking tray while still hot. The sugar will react with the baking soda and keep rising, and also darken to the beloved hokey-pokey colour. Leave it to cool for a few hours until it's at room temperature.

When cool, lay out a large sheet of baking paper on the bench and gently turn the brick of hokey pokey out on top of this. Chop the chocolate and melt it gently in a heatproof bowl set over a saucepan of simmering water. Paint the whole brick of hokey pokey with melted chocolate. Let the chocolate set, then break it up and serve!

RUM & RAISIN TRUFFLES

Recipe by **JONNY SCHWASS** *from Harlequin Public House*

MAKES: 30 | PREP TIME: 25 MINS, PLUS SOAKING AND CHILLING | COOK TIME: 40 MINS | SKILL LEVEL: 1 (EASY)

INGREDIENTS

½ cup (75 g) raisins
2 tbsp dark rum
200 g dark chocolate, chopped
30 g butter
½ cup cream
1 tsp orange zest
½ cup cocoa (or coconut or chopped roasted nuts)

GF

METHOD

Soak the raisins in the rum for 30 minutes. Combine the chocolate, butter and cream in a bowl, place over a pan of simmering water and warm until melted, stirring continuously.

When the chocolate mixture is smooth, add the rum-soaked raisins and any liquid, as well as the orange zest. Mix well and set aside to cool for 30 minutes, then chill for 4 hours or until firm enough to roll. Roll into walnut-sized balls, then roll in cocoa (or coconut or chopped roasted nuts). Keep in an airtight container in the fridge.

ULTIMATE BANANA FRITTERS

Recipe by **ANTHONY HOY FONG**

SERVINGS: 4–6 | PREP TIME: 10 MINS | COOK TIME: 30 MINS | SKILL LEVEL: 3 (CHALLENGING)

INGREDIENTS

200 g plain flour
125 g cornflour
½ tsp baking powder
1 tsp sugar
pinch of salt
250–300 ml club soda, ice cold
4 firm but ripe bananas
canola oil, for deep-frying
vanilla ice cream, to serve

Caramel
250 g sugar
¼ cup water

METHOD

To make the batter, sift flour, cornflour and baking powder into a large mixing bowl. Add sugar and salt. Make a well in the centre, then gradually pour the cold club soda in while whisking. This slowly incorporates the dry ingredients into the wet so as not to form any lumps.

Peel bananas and cut into quarters, on an angle, to create four obliquely cut bite-sized pieces. Add to batter and toss gently to coat evenly.

Heat oil, approximately 10 cm deep, in a large, heavy pot to 180°C. Working in small batches (so banana pieces don't stick together), carefully drop coated bananas into oil. Fry for 2–3 minutes while gently turning, until they puff up and become golden and crispy all over. Using a slotted spoon, remove and set aside on a wire rack set over paper towels.

Prepare caramel by placing sugar and water in a clean pot. Set over a high heat and simmer until sugar dissolves and liquid starts to turn a light amber colour – about 7–8 minutes. Prepare a large bowl of ice and water and set to one side.

Once caramel is a light amber colour, remove from heat immediately. Working quickly, take each piece of banana between two forks and drop into the caramel (be careful, as caramel will be extremely hot!). Toss to coat lightly all over, then transfer banana straight from the caramel into the bowl of ice water for 2–3 seconds, ensuring that you completely submerge it (this sets the caramel). Remove, drain and place on a plate. Repeat with remaining banana pieces. Serve while still hot in the centre, along with scoops of vanilla ice cream.

TIP

A good banana fritter needs to have warm, soft banana in the centre encased in a light, crispy batter. I emphasise the crispy texture on these traditional fritters with a light, hard caramel coating that gives it a distinctive 'snap' when you crack into it.

"When these are good, they're great – and when they're bad they're still pretty delicious!"

MERINGUES

Recipe by **JULIE LE CLERC**

MAKES: 16–20 | PREP TIME: 20 MINS | COOK TIME: 1½ HOURS | SKILL LEVEL: 1 (EASY)

INGREDIENTS

- 100 g (approx. 3) egg whites, at room temperature
- ¼ tsp cream of tartar
- 200 g (1 cup) caster sugar
- 1 tsp pure vanilla extract
- seasonal fruits and whipped cream, to serve

GF

METHOD

Pre-heat oven to 100°C. Line two oven trays with non-stick baking paper.

In a scrupulously clean bowl and using an electric mixer, whisk egg whites and cream of tartar together. Start whisking on low to create stabilising bubbles, then turn onto high and whisk until stiff peaks form.

Add 1 tablespoon of the measured sugar and whisk for 1 minute until the sugar has dissolved. Slowly add the remaining sugar, a tablespoonful at a time, and continue whisking until all the sugar is incorporated and dissolved and the mixture is very stiff, thick and glossy (this will take another 5 minutes). Test readiness by rubbing a little of the mixture between your fingers – it should feel silky smooth and not granular. Beat in the vanilla.

Using a large metal spoon, spoon mounds of meringue onto the prepared oven trays. Or pipe, using a large plain or star nozzle for different effects, if preferred. Leave space for the meringues to expand when cooked.

Bake for 90 minutes, until firm and dry. Don't be tempted to open the door before 90 minutes are up! Turn oven off and leave meringues in the oven to cool completely. This could ideally be done overnight.

Serve with fruits and dollops of cream.

Swirly alternatives: for swirly meringues, fold either ¼ cup melted dark chocolate or ¼ cup sieved raspberry purée through the finished meringue to create swirls of colour. Take care not to over-mix or the ripple effect will be lost. Shape and bake as instructed above.

TIP

I serve them with seasonal fruits and whipped cream.

"A light, crisp, white cloud of meringue is a beautiful thing to behold, and even nicer to eat."

RUSSIAN FUDGE

Recipe by **MICHELLE PATTISON**

MAKES: 30 LARGE SQUARES | PREP TIME: 1 HOUR | SKILL LEVEL: 2 (MODERATE)

INGREDIENTS

6 cups (1,250 g) sugar
1 cup milk
250 g butter
1 x 395 g tin sweetened condensed milk
2 tbsp golden syrup
2 tsp vanilla essence

GF

METHOD

Grease a tin 15 cm x 25 cm x 3.5 cm deep and line with non-stick baking paper. Set up an electric hand-mixer next to your stovetop, ready to go.

Pour sugar and milk into a medium-to-large saucepan and place over a medium heat. Stir continuously until combined and the sugar is dissolved.

Bring sugar syrup to the boil, then stir in butter, condensed milk, golden syrup and vanilla until combined. Stop stirring at this point and reduce the temperature slightly, to a simmer.

Monitor the temperature closely with a candy thermometer. When the colour starts to get darker (a caramel colour) and the temperature reaches 116°C degrees (soft-ball stage), remove from the heat.

Work quickly now. Place the hand-mixer into the hot fudge and beat continuously on quite a fast speed, until the fudge starts to lose its shine and look a bit dull (about 10–15 minutes). Using a scraper, pour fudge into the prepared tin. Continue to work quickly because it sets fast.

Allow fudge to cool completely and set, then remove from tin and cut into 5 cm x 5 cm squares. Store in an airtight container.

MANGAWHAI SEA SALT CARAMEL LOLLIPOPS

Recipe by **MARY BENNETT** *from Bennetts of Mangawhai*

MAKES: 15–20 | PREP TIME: 30 MINS, PLUS COOLING | SKILL LEVEL: 2 (MODERATE)

INGREDIENTS

200 g fresh cream
120 g liquid glucose
180 g sugar
30 g butter
1 tsp flaky sea salt
300 g dark or milk chocolate

GF

METHOD

To make the caramel: bring the cream to the boil in a saucepan. Meanwhile, in a separate saucepan, bring the glucose to the boil then slowly stir in the sugar.

When sugar is dissolved, continue boiling until a light caramel colour. Pour the hot cream in slowly and mix well. Continue cooking until the mixture reaches 119°C (firm-ball stage – see note below), mixing well all the time. Remove from the heat and add the butter and finally the salt.

To make the lollipops: pour the caramel into a baking tray lined with non-stick baking paper. When cool, cut into rectangular shapes. Press a stick into each rectangle.

To make the coating: break up chocolate and place in a stainless-steel bowl. Place the bowl over a pot of water. Simmer on a low heat, allowing chocolate to melt slowly for up to an hour. Do not allow water to boil.

Once chocolate is melted, remove bowl from the heat. Add the remaining chocolate pieces and stir in until dissolved. The chocolate will cool fairly quickly. When it is at body temperature, place the bowl back over the warm water. After a few minutes, dip the tip of a knife into the chocolate – if it sets smooth and glossy, the chocolate is tempered and ready to use.

Dip the lollipops into the chocolate, shake off any excess and place on a lined baking sheet to set.

NOTE

At firm-ball stage, a small amount of syrup dropped into very cold water forms a ball that holds its shape, but is still sticky, when pressed with your fingers.

"Buttery caramel is a favourite with so many kiwi kids, but these lollipops have a sophisticated spin that adults will also love."

CHOCOLATE MOUSSE WITH COFFEE GRANITA & CHOCOLATE TUILES

Recipe by **JACOB BROWN** *from The Larder*

SERVINGS: 10 | PREP TIME: 40 MINS, PLUS CHILLING & FREEZING
COOK TIME: 15–20 MINS | SKILL LEVEL: 2 (MODERATE)

INGREDIENTS

Mousse

300 g dark chocolate (70% cocoa solids)

5 egg yolks

2 eggs

250 g caster sugar

80 ml water

500 ml cream

Granita

about ½ cup caster sugar

1 litre weak black espresso coffee

Tuiles

85 g unsalted butter

1½ tbsp honey

165 ml plain flour

3 tsp cocoa powder

175 ml icing sugar

2 small egg whites

METHOD

For the mousse: melt chocolate in a double boiler or a heatproof bowl set over a pan of simmering water. Remove and allow to cool.

Beat egg yolks and eggs with an electric mixer until thick. While the mixture is rising in volume, combine sugar and water in a small saucepan and bring to the boil until it reaches the thread stage (120°C; see tip below). Carefully pour the boiling sugar mixture down the side of the bowl with the motor running and beat at a high speed for 10 minutes.

In a stainless-steel bowl, beat cream until soft peaks form. Fold melted chocolate into egg and sugar mix, then fold whipped cream into chocolate/egg mix until fully combined. Refrigerate in a suitable container for at least 2 hours or until set.

For the granita: add sugar to the coffee, to your taste. Pour liquid into a shallow metal tray and place in freezer. When it has just started to freeze, scrape with a fork to create granita flakes, and return to the freezer. Repeat scraping a few more times during freezing and again just before serving.

For the tuiles: in an electric mixer, cream butter and honey together. Add remaining ingredients and mix on a slow speed initially, then increase speed to high and mix for 5 minutes. Pour into a clean bowl and refrigerate for 1–2 hours.

Pre-heat oven to 150°C.

Spread batter paper-thin on sheets of baking paper to the desired shape (or roll batches of batter between two sheets of baking paper). Bake until light golden-brown and of a biscuit consistency, approximately 15–20 minutes. (If required, you can bend the tuiles into your desired shapes while still warm.) Place tuiles and baking paper on a wire rack to cool, and then store in an airtight container.

TIP

To check thread stage without a thermometer, drop a little syrup into a glass of cold water – it should form a liquid thread that does not ball up.

CHOCOLATE PANFORTE

Recipe by **GEOFF SCOTT** *from Vinnies*

MAKES: 1 | PREP TIME: 15 MINS, PLUS COOLING | COOK TIME: 35 MINS | SKILL LEVEL: 1 (EASY)

INGREDIENTS

350 g nuts – any mix of whole peeled almonds, skinned roasted hazelnuts, pistachios, walnuts
1 cup candied peel or other dried fruits
¾ cup (95 g) plain flour
4 tbsp Dutch cocoa powder, plus extra for dusting
zest of 1 orange
1 tsp ground cinnamon
2 tsp ground ginger
½ tsp ground cloves
½ tsp ground nutmeg
1 tsp freshly ground white pepper
90 g dark chocolate (70% cocoa solids), chopped
2 tbsp (30 g) butter
¾ cup (175 g) sugar
⅔ cup (175 g) honey
icing sugar, for dusting

METHOD

Pre-heat the oven to 150°C. Line the bottom of a 22 cm spring-form cake tin with baking paper. Spray the tin with baking spray, then dust the inside with cocoa. Make sure it covers the sides well.

In a mixing bowl, combine the nuts, candied peel, flour, cocoa, orange zest and all the spices, including pepper.

Place the chocolate in a small metal bowl and gently melt it over a pan of simmering water. Once melted, remove from the heat.

In a small saucepan, melt the butter, sugar and honey, stirring until the sugar dissolves, then bring to the boil and simmer for 3 minutes.

Working quickly, pour the hot honey syrup and melted chocolate over the nut mixture and stir well with a large metal spoon. Scrape the mix into the cake tin. Smooth the top with a rubber spatula or knife and press it flat.

Bake for 35 minutes. When done, the centre should be just set – be careful not to overcook it or it will become too hard. Place the tin on a wire rack for 30 minutes, then carefully remove the panforte and allow to cool completely before peeling away the baking paper.

Dust generously with icing sugar, then rub the icing sugar all over with your fingertips and dust again.

TIP

This panforte actually tastes better when it is left to 'mature' for at least a few days before eating.

"This panforte is normally served at Christmas time but is excellent all year round."

RASPBERRY ETON MESS

Recipe by **SHAUN CLOUSTON** *from Logan Brown*

SERVES: 4 | PREP TIME: 10 MINS | SKILL LEVEL: 1 (EASY)

INGREDIENTS

Raspberry purée

½ cup frozen raspberries

2 tbsp water

1 tbsp sugar

Eton mess

1 cup cream

½ cup plain or berry meringues (homemade or store-bought)

1 cup frozen raspberries

2 tbsp raspberry purée

GF

METHOD

Place raspberry purée ingredients in a microwavable bowl, cover and place in the juke box (microwave) for 2 minutes on medium. Remove from the microwave and pass through a fine sieve.

Whip the cream until soft peaks form. Crush the meringues. Crush the frozen raspberries while still frozen to break them up a bit.

Gently fold all the Eton mess ingredients together until they are just combined. Serve immediately, before the meringues soften too much.

CHOCOLATE ÉCLAIR WITH GANACHE & MACADAMIA BRITTLE

Recipe by **REX MORGAN** *from Boulcott Street Bistro*

SERVINGS: 15–18 | PREP TIME: 50 MINS | COOK TIME: 35 MINS | SKILL LEVEL: 3 (CHALLENGING)

INGREDIENTS

Éclairs

100 g butter

1 cup water

1 cup plain flour

3 large free-range eggs (size 7)

Chocolate ganache

100 ml cream

125 g good-quality dark chocolate, chopped

1 tbsp butter

Salted macadamia brittle

2 cups (270 g) roasted macadamia nuts

1 tsp salt

½ tsp baking soda

1¼ cups granulated sugar

⅓ cup water

75 g unsalted butter, at room temperature

To assemble

2 cups cream

METHOD

For the éclairs: pre-heat oven to 200°C. Grease two oven trays.

Bring butter and water to a rapid boil in a medium-sized saucepan. Remove from the heat and beat flour in with a wooden spoon, until the mixture leaves the side of the saucepan. Cool for a few minutes, then beat eggs in, one at a time, until mixture is smooth. You will need to use your muscles for this choux pastry.

Using a piping bag, with either a star or a plain nozzle, pipe 15 cm lengths of choux pastry, approximately 3 cm apart, on the greased oven trays. Bake for 20 minutes until puffed and light golden-brown. Reduce heat to 120°C, and bake for a further 15 minutes or so, to dry out and get a little more golden. Cool on a wire rack.

For the ganache: bring cream to the boil in a small saucepan. Place chocolate in a bowl, pour hot cream over and whisk with butter, until all dissolved and amalgamated. Set aside.

To make the brittle: pre-heat oven to 180°C. Place whole nuts on a baking tray. Place in oven. After 4 minutes, roll the nuts around on the tray and roast for another 4 minutes. Remove tray from oven and leave to cool. Coarsely chop nuts and mix with salt and baking soda. Coat a 30 cm x 43 cm shallow baking pan with vegetable oil or spray with non-stick cooking oil.

Put sugar and water in a medium-sized saucepan. Add the liquid glucose. Place over a medium heat, stir a little to mix, and bring to the boil. Continue boiling, undisturbed, until a layer of bubbles forms on top, about 3–4 minutes. Cover the pan, with the lid on a slight tilt, and continue to boil undisturbed for 5 minutes longer, until the brittle has turned a light caramel colour. Remove lid, add butter and gently stir with a wooden spoon a few times. When butter has melted and combined with the sugar mixture, cook over a medium heat until a sugar thermometer reads 150°C, about 8–10 minutes.

As soon as the sugar/butter mixture reaches the desired temperature, immediately but carefully stir nut mixture in. Using a long metal spatula, spread nut brittle as thinly and evenly as possible over the prepared pan. Leave to cool to room temperature; the brittle will harden very quickly.

When brittle is completely cooled and hardened, run a paper towel over the surface to absorb some of the oil. Carefully tap the brittle with a mallet or rolling pin to break it into crumbs. Store in an airtight container at cool room temperature.

To assemble: whip cream to stiff peaks and fold brittle through. Dip top half of each éclair into the ganache and leave, right-way-up, on a rack to set. If ganache has become too stiff, it can be softened by stirring over a small saucepan of simmering water. Once ganache is set, cut éclairs in half horizontally. Using a piping bag with a plain nozzle, pipe brittle cream into each base and place the lid on top to serve.

COCONUT & VANILLA ICE, ICE BABY

Recipe by **JONNY SCHWASS** *from Harlequin Public House*

MAKES: 20 PIECES | PREP TIME: 25 MINS, PLUS COOLING | SKILL LEVEL: 2 (MODERATE)

INGREDIENTS

100 g butter
1 cup milk
6 cups icing sugar
seeds from 1 vanilla pod
1 tsp salt
1 cup desiccated coconut
½ tsp coconut essence
1 tsp natural beetroot juice (optional)

GF

METHOD

Place the butter, milk, icing sugar, vanilla seeds and salt in a large saucepan and heat gently until the sugar dissolves. Bring the mixture to the boil and keep the heat sufficient to just maintain the boil, stirring only occasionally, until the mixture reaches soft-ball stage (116°C).

Add the coconut and coconut essence and remove from the heat. Cool for 5–10 minutes, then beat until the mixture thickens. Pour into a greased tin, approximately 20 cm x 20 cm. Allow to cool, then cut into squares. brown.

VARIATIONS

For a natural pink coconut ice, add beetroot juice with the coconut. For the traditional two-toned effect, divide the mixture in half before leaving to cool. Add ½ teaspoon of beetroot juice with half the coconut and essence to one half of mixture and beat until it starts to thicken. Spread into the tin. Add remaining coconut and essence to the other half, beat until it thickens and spread on top of the pink half. Allow to cool, then cut into squares.

"I wish I could say that this recipe was handed down to me by my grandmother on the birth of my first child, but it's actually inspired by the greatest hip-hop song ever recorded. When I hear the bass line from Queen's anthem 'Under Pressure', I, for one, will always stop, collaborate and listen."

ROCKY ROAD

Recipe by **HELEN JACKSON** *from Foodlovers*

MAKES: 40 CHUNKS | PREP TIME: 15 MINS, PLUS SETTING | COOK TIME: 10 MINS | SKILL LEVEL: 1 (EASY)

INGREDIENTS

750 g chocolate (I use a mixture of milk and dark)

1 cup (150 g) blanched peanuts

½ cup (60 g) pistachio nuts

½ cup (70 g) Brazil nuts, chopped roughly

¾ cup (65 g) dessicated coconut or coconut chips

180 g pink and white marshmallows

GF

METHOD

Pre-heat oven to 180°C. Grease or line a 20 cm x 25 cm slice tin.

Break chocolate into small pieces and place in a bowl set over a saucepan of barely simmering water. As soon as the chocolate starts to melt, turn the heat off, leave for a few minutes and then gently stir until smooth.

While chocolate is melting, place nuts in a baking dish and roast for around 8 minutes or until golden. Add coconut to the dish and toast for a further minute or two until the coconut is lightly coloured. Remove from the oven and set aside to cool.

Roughly chop marshmallows – kitchen scissors are good for this job.

Pour a thin layer of chocolate into the prepared slice tin and then cover with a layer of nuts, coconut and marshmallows. Cover with more chocolate and then remaining nuts, marshmallows and lastly all the remaining chocolate. Refrigerate to set and then chop into chunks.

VARIATIONS

You can vary your filling with the likes of crystallised ginger, jubes, dried fruit or chunks of shortbread.

"This festive treat is always popular and is very simple to make."

MINT TRUFFLES

Recipe by **MARY BENNETT** *from Bennetts of Mangawhai*

SERVINGS: 40 | PREP TIME: 2 ¾ HOURS, PLUS DRYING | SKILL LEVEL: 2 (MODERATE)

INGREDIENTS

Decoration

1 egg white

a few fresh mint leaves

1 tbsp caster sugar

Ganache

large handful of fresh mint leaves

200 g cream

80 g caster sugar

200 g Bennetts' dark chocolate

Coating

600 g Bennetts' dark chocolate

(GF)

METHOD

Start by making the decoration the day before. Whisk the egg white lightly with a fork. Dip mint leaves to coat both sides. Dust with caster sugar. Lay on a tray lined with baking paper and leave to dry overnight.

To make the ganache, place mint, cream and sugar in a saucepan. Bring to the boil, then turn off the heat. Allow to rest for 1 minute, or until satisfied with mint flavour, then discard the mint. Meanwhile, break the chocolate in pieces and put in a bowl. Pour the hot cream over and whisk until smooth and glossy. Allow to cool, then cover and place in the fridge until set. Scoop out teaspoons of the ganache, roll into round shapes and place the truffles on baking paper. Set aside.

To make the coating, break up chocolate and place 400 grams in a stainless-steel bowl. Place the bowl over a pot of water. Simmer on a low heat, allowing chocolate to melt slowly for up to an hour. Do not allow water to boil.

Once chocolate is melted, remove bowl from the heat. Add the remaining chocolate pieces and stir in until dissolved. The chocolate will cool fairly quickly. When it is at body temperature, place the bowl back over the warm water. After a few minutes, dip the tip of a knife into the chocolate – if it sets smooth and glossy, the chocolate is tempered and ready to use.

With the help of a fork, dip the truffles one by one into the chocolate, shake off excess chocolate, and place on baking paper in the fridge for 15–20 minutes until set. To finish, decorate with pieces of candied mint leaf. A drop of liquid chocolate helps the decoration stick to the truffle.

TIPS

Rolling truffles is a messy business, so dip your hands in cocoa powder every so often. When melting the chocolate, the bowl must not touch the simmering water below.

"As a chocolate lover I don't obsess about the percentage of cocoa solids – as long as it's good, that's what matters to me."

SALTED ALMOND BLACK SESAME BRITTLE

Recipe by **PETER GORDON**

MAKES: ABOUT 300 G | PREP TIME: 15 MINS | SKILL LEVEL: 2 (MODERATE)

INGREDIENTS

100 g flaked almonds
2 tbsp black sesame seeds
¼ tsp flaky salt
200 g caster sugar

DF GF

METHOD

Pre-heat oven to 160°C.

Lay a sheet of baking paper on a baking tray that has no sides. Spread almonds over the tray and toast in the oven until they turn golden-brown (6–8 minutes). Cool. Mix almonds with sesame seeds and salt.

Place sugar in a clean, dry, medium-sized saucepan and melt over a medium heat without stirring. You can shake the pan gently to ensure it melts and colours evenly, but don't stir because if the sugar crystallises, you'll have to start again.

Once the sugar has turned dark golden in colour, turn off the heat and add the almond mixture. Carefully stir to coat the almonds with caramel, then tip onto the baking paper. Work quickly now as the sugar sets.

Lay another sheet of paper on top, then roll the brittle out with a rolling pin while still hot – make it as thin as you can. Leave to cool, then peel away the paper, break into pieces and store in an airtight container.

HOKEY POKEY ICY SLICEYS WITH SALTED CARAMEL SAUCE

Recipe by **GEOFF SCOTT** *from Vinnies*

SERVINGS: 10 | PREP TIME: 30 MINS, PLUS FREEZING | COOK TIME: 10 MINS | SKILL LEVEL: 2 (MODERATE)

INGREDIENTS

2 litres hokey pokey ice cream
180 g butter
180 g brown sugar
1 tsp vanilla extract
2 eggs
220 g plain flour
220 g wholemeal flour
1 tsp baking powder
½ tsp bicarbonate of soda
1 x 380 g tin caramel sweetened condensed milk

Salted caramel sauce
125 ml water
125 g sugar
125 ml cream
1 tsp salt

METHOD

Line a 20 cm x 30 cm slice tin with greaseproof paper. Tip ice cream into tin and press down flat, then freeze until hard. Use an 8 cm plain cookie cutter to cut 10 rounds and re-freeze.

Pre-heat the oven to 180°C. Cream butter, sugar and vanilla together in a food processor, then add eggs and mix. Add flours, baking powder and bicarbonate of soda, and mix to combine and form a dough.

Split dough in half, and roll each half out to 4 mm thick. Place on baking trays lined with baking paper and rest in the fridge for 30 minutes. Use a 9 cm crinkle cookie cutter to cut 20 rounds, placing back on the trays on fresh baking paper. Cook for 10 minutes until golden, then remove to a rack to cool.

For the salted caramel sauce, bring water and sugar to the boil and cook until the syrup begins to turn golden. In a separate saucepan, gently heat cream. Take caramel-coloured sugar off the heat and carefully whisk in the hot cream. Stir salt in.

To assemble, spread half the biscuits with caramelised condensed milk, place ice cream rounds on top and finish with a biscuit lid. Dip into lightly warmed salted caramel sauce or drizzle it over.

TIPS

The ice cream is best left overnight to freeze solid. Have pre-cut ice cream rounds laid out on plastic wrap in the freezer to make for quick assembly and easy serving.

"To me, food is all about tasting something delicious, having a laugh and sharing the moment with friends. For a little bit of nostalgia and fun, try this twist on the great hokey pokey icy slicey."

MOONSHINE BIFF (MARSHMALLOW)

Recipe by **DAVID GRIFFITHS** *from Mister D*

SERVINGS: 16–20 | PREP TIME: 20 MINS, PLUS CHILLING | SKILL LEVEL: 1 (EASY)

INGREDIENTS

450 g sugar
450 ml water
4 tbsp powdered gelatine
240 g icing sugar
3 capfuls rum
2 tsp vanilla paste
50 g desiccated coconut

DF GF

METHOD

Bring sugar, water and gelatine to the boil in a pot and let simmer for 8 minutes. Place in the bowl of an electric mixer and whisk on high for 3 minutes. Add icing sugar, rum and vanilla, and whisk on high for another 5 minutes, until light and fluffy.

Place in a lightly greased tray to required thickness and allow to set in the fridge for 2–4 hours.

Place coconut on a roasting tray under a medium–hot oven grill for 30 seconds at a time, stirring repeatedly until golden. Watch it like a hawk – coconut will burn quickly if unattended. Allow to cool, then cut biff into cubes or rectangles and coat with coconut.

"I guess every Dad has his party dish – this was Jim's."

CHOCOLATE FUDGE CAKE

Recipe by **SAM MANNERING** *from Homestead*

SERVINGS: 6–8 | PREP TIME: 15 MINS, PLUS SOAKING & CHILLING | SKILL LEVEL: 1 (EASY)

INGREDIENTS

Cake

½ cup currants or raisins
2 tbsp whisky or sherry
120 g butter
120 g brown sugar
1 tbsp cocoa powder
1 x 250 g packet Wine Biscuits
1 egg, beaten lightly
½ cup walnuts, chopped roughly

Icing

60 g butter, softened
1½ cups icing sugar
2 tbsp good-quality dark cocoa powder
1 tbsp water (approx.)

METHOD

Soak the currants in the whisky or sherry for an hour. In a saucepan over a low-ish heat, melt together the butter and brown sugar. Remove from the heat and stir in the cocoa.

Crush the biscuits well with a rolling pin or in a blender. Add to the saucepan, together with the currants/raisins, beaten egg, and walnuts, and mix in until everything is combined.

Take a slice or loaf tin, grease well and line with baking paper. Fill with the mixture, smoothing down with the back of a spoon.

To make the icing, beat the butter with the icing sugar and cocoa, adding up to 1 tablespoon of water to get a nice smooth consistency. Spread the icing over the base, cover and refrigerate for at least 3 hours, until everything is set. Cut into small squares and demolish.

"Every time I have a piece, I feel like I'm about eight years old and the adults are having after-dinner coffee, and I'm about to get in trouble because I should be in bed but I'm not – I'm out to sneak a bit of this stuff! It's a little bit rich, a little bit boozy, a little bit easy to make."

I LIKE-A LIKE-A LOLLY CAKE

Recipe by **JONNY SCHWASS** *from Harlequin Public House*

MAKES: 1 x 30 CM CAKE | PREP TIME: 15 MINS, PLUS CHILLING | COOK TIME: 40 MINS | SKILL LEVEL: 1 (EASY)

INGREDIENTS

20 g butter
200 g sweetened condensed milk
190 g Eskimo lollies
1 x 250 g malt biscuits
1 cup desiccated coconut

METHOD

In a medium-sized saucepan, warm butter and condensed milk, stirring to mix. Remove from the heat.

Cut Eskimo lollies into bite-sized chunks. Crush biscuits to crumbs in a food processor.

In a large bowl, mix butter and condensed milk with crushed biscuits and chopped lollies. Form into a log shape and roll in coconut. Enclose log in plastic wrap and chill in fridge for 4 hours.

When set, cut into slices and enjoy!

"Eat with your kids (or when you feel like being a kid again)."

INDEX

(DF) = DAIRY FREE (GF) = GLUTEN FREE

Page numbers in italics refer to photographs.

DESSERTS

DOUGH & PASTRY BASICS

ICINGS, FILLINGS & TOPPINGS

FRITTERS

GLUTEN FREE

ICE CREAM & GRANITA

LOAVES & BREADS

VEGETARIAN – SWEET

CONTRIBUTORS

ACKNOWLEDGEMENTS

Thank you to Steve Anderson, Craig Atkinson, Steve Bayliss, Cara Bayly, Toni Brandso, Rachel Byars, Rebecca Clouston, Mary Direen, Helen Emett, Rod Gibson, Mark Hamilton, Athalia Harper, Hayden Harvey, Lyle Hastings, Joan Mackenzie, Jocelyn McCallum, Creghan Molloy-Wright, Dave Patience, Anne Thom, Sam Thom, Angie and Madeline Tipping, Mike Tod, Karl van Wynbergen and Mary Wells for your support.

Thank you to Constance from Dove Cote in Mission Bay, Emma and John from Tile Space in Parnell, Jennie French, Dale and Melinda Garratt, the team at Le Monde in Parnell, Lisa from Nest in Grafton, the team at Stevens St Lukes and Lianne Whorwood for kindly supplying additional props.

Thank you to Catherine Belcher, Liv Buchanan, Pearl Harper, Liv Patience and the Pattison Family for allowing us into your lovely homes.

We would also like to extend special thanks to the following organisations for their invaluable assistance in making *The Great New Zealand Baking Book*:

Air New Zealand Limited, Bell Tea Company and Foodstuffs (N.Z.) Limited

The Great New Zealand Baking Book benefits New Zealand charity KidsCan, which will receive a portion of the proceeds to support their inspired efforts toward supporting disadvantaged kiwi kids: kidscan.org.nz

Find and follow us on:
#thegreatnzbakingcookbook
thegreatnewzealandbakingbook.co.nz

ISBN: 978-0-473-33963-0
Printed in China by 1010 Printing Group Limited
10 9 8 7 6 5 4 3 2 1

PUBLISHER: Geoff Blackwell
EDITOR IN CHIEF: Ruth Hobday
EXECUTIVE PRODUCER: Murray Thom
CREATIVE DIRECTOR: Tim Harper
PRODUCER: Wendy Nixon
DESIGN: Tim Harper, Bridget White
PHOTOGRAPHY: Lottie Hedley
VIDEOGRAPHY: Hayley Thom
HEAD BAKER: Michelle Pattison
PROJECT EDITOR: Abby Aitcheson
FOOD EDITOR: Teresa McIntyre
ADDITIONAL EDITORIAL: Mary Dobbyn, Susan Brookes
ADDITIONAL PRODUCTION: Jenny Moore

ORIGINAL CONCEPT CREATED BY:
Murray Thom and Tim Harper